The Courage of Grace

MAP
Kansas City (MO)

The Courage of Grace

Thoughts of Reclaiming the Christian Royalty

Marie-Tudor A. Arrey

The Courage of Grace
Marie-Tudor Arrey

Published by
Miraclaire Academic Publications (MAP)
Kansas City, MO 64138, USA

Copyright © 2013 by MAP

All rights for this book reserved.
No part of this book may be reproduced, stored in a retrieval system, or transmitted, in any form or by any means, electronic, mechanical, photocopying, recording or otherwise, without the prior permission of the copyright owner.

ISBN-13: 978-0615823614 / ISBN-10: 0615823610

MAP is an imprint of Miraclaire Publishing LLC
www.miraclairepublishing.com

Printed in the United States of America

Miraclaire Publishing makes every effort to ensure the accuracy of all the information ("Content") in its publications. However, Miraclaire and its agents and licensors make no representations or warranties whatsoever as to the accuracy, completeness, or suitability for any purpose of the Content and disclaim all such representations and warranties, whether expressed or implied to the maximum extent permitted by law. Any views expressed in this publication are the views of the author and are not necessarily the views of Miraclaire.

ACKNOWLEDGEMENTS

To My Lord Jesus: thank you for the beautiful life that you have given me. I love you more! To Pastor Obi Victor Itambon and Pastor Mercy Obi, you have given my life a meaning, opened my eyes to endless possibilities and opportunities and brought meaning to the thoughts in my heart. I will not wait for heaven to thank you. I love you very much! To my colleagues at Hermes Institution, Powerbache Institution and Diamond Centre Institution thank you all. Thanks to all the pastors of Faith family fellowship international. To my dad, mum, and my entire family - you are the best. To all my friends, brethren and students, thank you and God bless you all.

WHY I WROTE THIS BOOK

The Courage of Grace: Thoughts of Reclaiming the Christians Royalty. Who will dare pen her thoughts, assessments and interpretation of such controversial topic during these days of errors? A time and period where people no longer want to make God's word the standard for their life. The revelation and conviction were strong enough and compelled me to write this book carefully and cautiously. The mixture and misunderstanding of God's word by some church-goers pushed me to put down my thoughts in writing. I am certain that these thoughts will be made manifest in your life as you read through this book in Jesus' name. Read and enjoy.

Marie-Tudor A. Arrey

Table of Contents

Acknowledgements i
Why I Wrote this Book ii

GENERAL INTRODUCTION 1

CHAPTER ONE
COURAGE AND GRACE 4

CHAPTER TWO
THE PRICE TO PAY 20

CHAPTER THREE
SOME FALLEN CHRISTIAN VALUES IN THIS DISPENSATION OF GRACE 32

CHAPTER FOUR
THE GIANT AND HIS SOURCES OF STRENGTH 43

CHAPTER FIVE
STRATEGIES TO ADOPT TO DEFEAT YOUR GIANTS 55

CHAPTER SIX
REWARDS FOR ROYALTY 70

CHAPTER SEVEN
MILK AND HONEY 80

Bibliography 90

GENERAL INTRODUCTION

In order to get the best out of ourselves, we are encouraged to be firm in our faith with God. For this to be fulfilled we need to depend on the Almighty God who has everything it takes to make us arrive at our objectives in life. Many people think they own their lives. It is not true. God is the owner of our lives. (Galatians 2:20-21)

For us to live is Christ because He bought us with an expensive price. We all were condemned of the sin of disobedient of our fore parents Adam and Eve. Like sheep, we all went astray and the loving kindness of our heavenly Father sorts us out of darkness.

If our heavenly Father had such pity on us and saved us, it therefore means that His thoughts for us are thoughts of good and not of evil to bring us to an expected end. (Jeremiah 29:11) If somebody is concerned about your welfare, it means the person will do his best to make you live a fulfilled and happy life. To this cause moving ahead and taking the first place in this life requires our continuous reliance on the Almighty God.

Being on the top, means looking unto God, and taking instruction from Him. The tragedy today is that many people want to be at the top without obeying God's instruction. In life if God is not the one leading you, then obviously, the devil will be the one leading you. You cannot claim to be a member of a family and disobey the rules and regulations binding the family and you expect to be blessed by the head of the family. Disobeying the head of the family is indirectly informing the head of the family that you can make it on your own.

For every throne you will intend to possess there is a giant on your way so be prepared to defeat him. If you do not have, what it takes to overcome the giant you will fail from accomplishing your objective. What it takes to win is faith in God. If you do not have this, your giant will defeat and torment you and if care is not taken you will live a life without a sense of direction.

It is the desire of the enemy to see you frustrated, tormented and discouraged with life. If he succeeds in doing this to you, he has succeeded having you as his servant without negotiating with you. In this dispensation, people are looking for courageous leaders who would flinch from difficult situations; leaders who would put up with their responsibilities come rain come sun.

Therefore, get all you need to overcome your giant, the Lord is on your side, He will see you through as long as you keep faith in God. For you to make it in life and defeat the giant on your way, you need the God factor. Having the God factor, means you must be determined to walk according to the precepts of God Almighty, so that when you are confronted with the giant on your way to your throne, you will rise up and challenge him with courage and by the grace of God. Remember God is with you, and so, power, victory, and glory are yours. You cannot afford to fail. God will give you a favourable answer. He is the one that gives us grace and courage to overcome and win in a situation of despair. Rise up and take your position at the top.

CHAPTER ONE
COURAGE AND GRACE

The Potency of Courage

Nelson Mandela the former South African Stateman and Nobel peace winner said "*I learned that courage was not the absence of fear, but the triumph over it. The brave man is not he who does not feel afraid, but he who conquers that fear.*"

This courage has been defined as the quality of mind or spirit that makes a person able to control fear in the face of damage, danger, hardship, pain and misfortune. It is the ability to control fear and triumph over it, not the absence of fear. Courage is the ability to stand in the midst of a fearful situation. In the book of Joshua found in the Bible, God told Joshua at the commencement of his leadership responsibilities to be courageous. People are looking for leaders who are able to stand against all odds, one that is ready to sail through wavy storms and thundering circumstances victoriously.

The race of life is not free from problems so for you to rise above problems the virtue of courage is necessity. Courage is the virtue that people ought to develop to help them fight and overcome their daily battles. It is an ingredient needed to face life's challenges. The Bible encourages us to fear not, but to be courageous. Many are so fearful that they allow their circumstances or situation to overcome them not because the situation or problem was more than them to tackle, but because they permitted Mr "Fear" to take hold and grip them. Nevertheless, the Lord Himself says FEAR NOT. The spirit of fear gripped even John the apostle at a point in his life, but the Lord encouraged him not to be afraid.

> *"And when I saw Him I fell at his feet as dead. And He laid his right hand upon me, saying unto me, fear not; I am the first and the last, I am He that liveth, and was dead; and behold, I am alive for evermore, Amen; and have the keys of hell and death"* (Revelation 1:17-18)

Courage is not daring in a situation, problem, or circumstance which you know the word of God is contrary and yet you go along to dare. In such a case if anything negative happens to you, you will be blamed for not being knowledgeable. For example, somebody goes and climbs on a story building and decides to jump down, saying God will send His angels to help him, down. This is tempting God, and if such an intentional act is done in the name of courage, what awaits such an individual is disaster.

On the other hand, if you found yourself on top of a story building, let's say trying to escape an enemy's attack and you cry out to God for deliverance, He will bring deliverance. Your being there, and having no escape route, and yet you desire to escape his attack, will bring about the Lord's intervention in a unique way beyond your understanding. God knows how to deliver you from such an attack.

Courage can be seen in the life of a young boy or girl who wrote an entrance exam and succeeded. When it was time to go for the orals, which he succeeded, but was, requested a sum of money, for his name to appear on the final list. With courage he refuses to give the amount of money they requested, saying "it is a sin against the Lord God; saying he will not dare to do such a thing against the Lord. This is courage in action because not everybody will attempt to refuse such an offer.

People, who do not have value for God's Kingdom, will see such a person as dull, stupid foolish etc. but such an individual has been approved by God for standing his ground and this act will bring glory to God.

Despite the odds he will face because of refusing to give bribe, this will not bother him because he knows it is only for a while and the Lord will change the story. There are many Biblical examples whereby some heroes of old demonstrated courage. Let us see the case of the three Hebrew boys, Shadrack, Meshach and Abednego who refused to bow to the golden image which every other person in the town bowed. King Nebuchadnezzar commanded the mightiest men to bind the three boys and throw them into the burning fiery for disobeying to bow before the image. When he commanded that the boys be thrown inside the furnace, he first came and inquired from them if they were willing to change their mind and bow to the golden image so that their lives will be spared.

In replied they told the Kind that even if God whom they serve does not deliver them, they will not bow down to that golden image which has been set up as a god. In the furnace of fire, a fourth Man appeared with them and the flame did not consume them. The same way these Hebrew boys refused to compromise and they were delivered, your case will not be different if you stand your grounds.

In that difficult situation which you now found yourself because you refused to be a part in given bribe, idol worshipping, and the marring of peoples images, and you are being persecuted for that, the Lord will visit you and your story will be that of victory in Jesus' Name. You who is exercising courage in that fearful situation you find yourself in, and some people are telling you to compromise and get it the cheap way, yet you have stood your ground on what is right, I have this song to encourage you to keep standing.

1. Courage, brethren! Do not stumble
   Though thy path be dark as night
   There's a star to guide the humble
   Trust in God and do the right.

2. Let the road be rough and dreary
   And its end far out of sight
   Foot it bravely, strong or weary
   Trust in God, and do the right.

3. Perish policy and cunning
   Perish all that fear the light
   Whether losing whether winning
   Trust in God, and do the right.

4. Trust no party sect or fraction
   Trust no leader in the fight
   But in every word and action

Trust in God, and do the right

5. Trust no lovely form of passion
   Friends may look like angels bright,
   Trust no custom, school or fashion,
   Trust in God and do the right.

6. Simple rule, and safest guiding;
   Inward peace and inward might;
   Star upon our path abiding
   Trust in God and do the right.

Grace Within

Somebody recently asked God in despair: "Lord, I try to love you with all my heart. I stand on your promises and believe you want to bless me. Why isn't anything happening?" He answered, "You are struck where you are because you have failed to use the grace I have placed within you to appropriate my riches and overcome." This confused the person because she has always thought God's grace and blessings were the same thing... something you asked for and He handed out.

Actually God works to bless us in two different ways. He works for us from the outside, and He works within us, helping us to exercise His power and to lay hold of His riches. Sadly, some Christians get struck on what they want God to do for them, and ignore the powerful works of grace He wants to accomplish from within.

PastorMorris Cerullo has often said that *"It's time for the Church to move beyond the point of blessing, receiving what God can do for you, into the realm of power by realizing what He wants to do with you through the active force of grace."*

Paul knew God's grace as a force: "and he said by the grace of God, I am what I am, and His grace to me was not without effect. No, I worked harder than all of them-yet not I, but the grace of God that was with me" (1Corinthians15:10, NIV)

God's grace is an active force within you. Exercise it, lay hold of it today, and you will enter a new realm of power and blessings.

What is Grace?

Grace means enabling power, it is also the supernatural ability given to a person, to accomplish a task. The apostle Paul was given grace for ministration to the Gentile while the apostle Peter was given ministerial grace to Jews. (Galatians2:7-9) Every child of God has ability and an area of grace he/she can best function. What to do is to locate your area of grace and your life will never be the same.

> *"For the grace of God that bringeth salvation halt appeared to all men, teaching us that denying ungodliness and worldly lusts, we should live soberly, righteously and Godly, in this present world, looking for that blesseth hope, and the glorious appearing of the great God and our savior Jesus Christ who gave Himself for us, that He might redeem us from all iniquity (sin)and purity unto himself a peculiar people zealous of good work." Titus 2:11-14*

Grace brought us salvation free. No amount of money were we charged to pay in order to be saved.

Grace did it for us and we are commanded to live lives pleasing to God. Grace will not come to effect where there is willing ignorant. Grace will come to effect in that area where we are unable to do that God given assignment, which when we do, our fulfillment will come to effect. This does not seem to be the message of some religious institutions. You are called to live godly, righteous, holy and pure and grace is the enabler to do this. Grace is God working in us to conform us to Christ's image. Jesus walked in God's grace. (Luke 2:40) if this is not where we are heading, then we are deceived and heading towards the opposite of salvation. The Holy Spirit works on us to accomplish this deeming difficult list of godly expectations. In living our faith daily and obeying, we produce good works acceptable to God. Works do not save us because our dependence is upon God. They are just the inevitable result of a true relationship with God.

When Grace is at work in a Christian's life
God uses the weak things to confront the wise. The Grace of God is also referred to as the hand of God. When a person acknowledges his inadequacy, to carry out that God given assignment the grace of God will come to that person's life and work in the area concerned. When you discover your area of grace, you will function without stress. Everybody can sing but not everybody has the gift of singing. When somebody with the gift of singing sings, he does it without stress. This is because he has discovered his area. Grace will enable you to function properly in the area where you are gifted.

Things that God's Grace will do in your life
- Grace will cause you to excel in every good work. 2Corinthians 8:6-7
- Grace brings guarantee of what God has spoken to you. Romans 4:16
- Grace helps you operate in the supernatural. Act6:8-10
- Grace makes you to become what you were born for or makes you to fulfill your destiny. Acts 4:33-34
- Grace makes you to function in your area of assignment. Acts 4:33-34
- Grace strengths you spiritually and physically. 2Corinthians 12:9
- Grace makes people see the supernatural wonders at work in the life of an individual person considered weak. 1Corinthians15:10
- Grace will celebrate you and cause you to do exploit in your area of assignment. Acts 14:26, 2:9)
- We are gifted in different areas; therefore grace differs from one man to the other. Romans12:6

When Grace is Absent

We gave another definition of grace as God in the race. The G stands for God and R stands for race. This therefore means when grace is absent, you experience disgrace. People will not tolerate you, and you will be exposed. When grace is not at work, you will put in much labour and get very little profit and the reverse will happen to you when grace is at work.

Some people use God's grace and forgiveness as a license to live in sin. They have all sorts of excuses and persuasive arguments to ignore God's word. And some just say, grace reigns unto eternal life. When some religious leaders who love darkness, turn to explain grace in this way, you have to be watchful and careful not to be misled.

> *"For there are certain men who crept in unaware, who were before of old ordained to this condemnation, ungodly men, turning the grace of our God into lasciviousness, and denying the only God, and our Lord Jesus Christ." Jude 4*

Turning grace into licence to sin is the same as denying Jesus. This brings shame upon everything the cross represented. When you do this, you will be referred to as someone whose heart has been blinded. For those who shine the light on sin will be called to judgment for they must be ashamed for turning the light off. Sinners and hypocrites find comfort in darkness. You as a Christian desiring to please and walk according to God's standard, do not be a part to such.

Grace is the divine influence on the heart and its reflection is shown in your life. Grace enables you to live a life pleasing to God. Grace will cause you to abound in every good work. (2Corinthians 9:8) Grace pardons and cleanse within. Grace was given to us by God, therefore it is our inheritance, as Christians. (2Thessalonian 1:1) Grace is not a covering for unrighteousness as it has been presented by some people who claim to be Christians. "For the law was given by Moses, but grace and truth came by Jesus Christ" (John1:17)

Grace enables us to live in the intent of the law as unfolding by the Spirit. The word reveals that the Lord restores us and leads us in paths of righteousness for His name sake (Psalms23:3) It will be very dangerous on our part to suppose that the Lord overlooks our continued sinfulness and love of darkness for His name sake, yet this is the predominant religious message to some men. Where is the restoration in such evil practices? This example will help us to work out our salvation with fear and tremble.

> *"I will therefore put you in remembrance, though ye once knew this, how that the Lord, having saved the people out of the land of Egypt, afterward destroyed them that believed not" Jude5*

The scripture above is referring to those children of Israel who after seeing all the great miracles of God, like the judgment He brought on Egypt on their behalf, the parting of the red sea, Manna which He fed them with, and water from the rock, they did not put the slightest bit of faith in Him (Deuteronomy 4:33-36). The spiritual rock, from which they spiritually drank and that followed them was Christ. (Psalms 105:41, 1Corinthians 10:4) They rejected Him. They only thought of themselves, on what they would eat or drink and the types of food they wanted. (Exodus 16:2-3, Number 11:5-6) They were also idolatrous.

> *"But with many of them, God was not well pleased; for they were overthrown in the wilderness. Now these things were our examples to the intent we should not lust after evil things as they also lusted. Neither be ye idolaters, as it is written, the* people sat down

to eat and drink and rose up to play" 1Corinthians 10:5-7

They tempted God and many were destroyed. (Number 11:1, 10:33, 14:4 Deuteronomy 9:7-8) We must take heed lest we fall (1Corinthians 10:9-12) (Hebrews 3:16-19) They ate and drank of God's table and then went out to play in their flesh (lust, desires, Man's will) They also constantly wanted to return to the bondages of Egypt from which God had delivered them. They even made false gods to go before them (Exodus 32:34).

This is highly representative of those who make a commitments with God's grace as justification for continuing in wrong doing. "For if I build again the things which I destroyed, I made myself a transgressor." Galatians 2:18 they actually served another god, a golden calf of their own making. God said they were stiff-necked (rebellions) and stiff-hearted and that they would not enter into His promised land. (salvation) Number14:23, 32:11, 13, Deuteronomy 2:14-16) Those who are rebellious to God's will and refuse to follow God's standards, will not enter into heaven. Do you see the correlation? They did not continue in God's covenant and He disregarded them. (Hebrew8:9) God said they were a stubborn and rebellion generation that set not their heart aright, and their spirit was not steadfast with God. (Psalms78:8, Psalms 78:36-37)

"Nevertheless they did flatter Him with their mouth, and they lied unto Him with their tongues. For their heart was not right before Him, neither were they steadfast in His covenant." They said one thing and did another – their hearts were not on God – just a desire for His blessings. Many will profess Christ, yet seek their own. Please take note and pay attention to this not, to repeat their errors.

They sent out spies that brought back a bad report. They said the people were many, they lived in walled cities, and there were giants in the land. (Number13:28-33, Deuteronomy1:28) God said that He would be the one to fight the battles, and they should not be moved. (Number10:9, 14:9, Deuteronomy1:30) They rejected God's counsel because of their worry and lack of faith. As they spoke in God's ears, so He did to them (Number14:28) AS such, God suffered them to wander in the wilderness until that whole generation dropped dead.

The correlation is this: some religious men will tell you that you cannot live without sinning, sin abounds, bad thoughts, bad deeds, there will be high walls, do as you like. Do not listen to their advice.

Jesus says I have provided my Spirit and will give you the strength and power you need to fight the battles. (Hebrews 1:9) He says we should put faith in Him and the victory over those negative situations will be our portion. The book of Titus has this "who gave Himself for us that He might redeem us from all iniquity, and purify unto Himself a peculiar people, zealous of good works." Titus 2:14

Just like in the days of old it will not be different from anyone who refuses to serve the Lord in integrity and sincerity of heart. The children of Israel in the days of old erred greatly. And the Lord made mention that for forty years long was He grieved with this generation, and said, they were people that do err in their heart and they have not known His ways. Unto them, God swore in His wrath that they will not enter into His rest." If you lack faith, you can then make this prayer by saying, Oh Lord I believe, help my unbelief (Mark 9:24, Luke17:5, Hebrews 3:12,19) God said, those who did not rebel against Him would enter into the promised Land. (Number14:30-31)

How the Lord leads by Grace

How the Lord leads- symbolic of Christ. (Psalms107:7) God led the children of Israel as a pillar of cloud by day and a pillar of fire by night. (Exodus13:21-22, Number9:16-23, Psalms78:14) "yet thou in thy manifold mercies forsook them not in the wilderness. The pillar of cloud departed not from them by day to lead them in the way, neither the pillar of fire departed by night to show them light and the way wherein they should go" Jesus is the pillar we follow, for He is the light . (Isaiah60:1, Luke 1:79, John1:4-5) "And the way" (Matthew7:14, Matthew10:52, Luke20:21, John14:4,6) The Lord led His own people to go forth like sheep, and guided them in the wilderness like flock."

Today, His grace is leading us through a righteous path and it will not be in vain. For those who are living their lives anyhow and are saying we are in the dispensation of grace, let's do it anyhow, will reap a disastrous reward when their cup must have been full. Grace can be very good when we apply it in our good relationship with Christ, by living according to His standard, and it can also be very dangerous if we take the grace of God for granted.

In the days of old, some children of God had identification with God, but not a heart to do His will.

Only a remnant actually entered into the Promised Land. Jesus the good shepherd also leads His sheep (John10:14, Isaiah 40:11) and He shall feed His flock like a shepherd: He shall gather the lambs with His arm and carry them in his bosom and shall gently lead those that are His. Similarly, the rebellious may abstractly identify with Christ, but will be separated and not enter into eternal life. (Matthew 25:32-33) Just as the Israelites followed the pillar of cloud, we must follow and obey God, as He leads and remain faithful Christians.

Flesh or Spirit
"For if ye live after the flesh ye shall die, but if ye through the Spirit do mortify (put to death) the deeds of the body, ye shall live," Romans 8:13 You are to deny the flesh and feed the Spirit with the word of God for you to live in conformity with Christ. Living in the flesh is doing those things that are contrary to God's will, this include worldliness, and the putting of self above God. Something will always happen when you glorify the flesh above God. It could be you are feeding the flesh on a constant base while neglecting the Spirit. This could be getting involved with carnal activities which are contrary to the word of God. Neglecting to feed our Spirit with the Word of God can bring about many negative things in our life.

The Endless Possibilities of the Flesh
The possibilities of the flesh are endless. The flesh wants what it wants, when it wants, while the spirit is sacrificing and patient. The flesh wants to do what is right in its own eye regardless of others. While the

spirit denies itself for the benefit of others (love). The flesh takes, the spirit gives. The flesh exalt itself, the spirit is humble. The flesh wants to corrupt; the spirit wants to set things done in the right manner according to the will of God. "For he that soweth to his flesh shall of the flesh reap corruption, but he that soweth to the spirit shall of the spirit reap everlasting life" Galatians6:8.

We must examine ourselves and make up our mind to be true followers of Christ. It is one thing to be in Christ Jesus, and another thing to walk according to the leadership of the Spirit. For such there is no condemnation. (Romans 8:1) If you are a Christian, and you are sowing to the flesh, then do not assume God's grace allows it. Christ's death was a precious thing and if you are using God's grace as a licence to continue in wrong doing, then have it at the back of your mind that you are only deceiving yourself. God cannot be mocked. A man will only harvest what he sows. Those who «profess» Christ yet continue to live in sin are greatly fooling themselves. This is what Apostle Paul said in the book of Galatians. "This I say walk in the spirit and ye shall not fulfill the lust of the flesh. Galatians 5:16

Ways to Discover your Area of Grace
- ➢ Those things you love doing. For example, to some people singing for an hour is really a burden. Whereas others could sing for the next two hours and yet enjoy doing it. Those who enjoy doing it, are said to have grace in music. The same can be applicable to our different areas of grace. It could be teaching, driving, preaching, counseling etc…..

> Those things you do naturally without stress and without straining.
> Those things you can grade yourself one hundred percent.
> Those things people say and enjoy about your personality.
> Those things you can do without payment, and yet you still derive satisfaction from doing it.
> You can also discover your area of grace through prayer.

God loves you and wants to answer your prayer. You can make this prayer. Heavenly Father, thank you for awakening me to your grace as a powerful force within me. I long to grow beyond the point of blessing and into the realm of power! , Help me to exercise Your grace, so I might lay hold of all You have for me. In Jesus name, Amen.

CHAPTER TWO
THE PRICE TO PAY

"Then said Jesus unto His disciples, if any man will come after me, let him deny himself, and take up his cross, and follow me" For whosoever desires to save his life will lose it, and whosoever loses his life for my sake will find it. "For what profit is it to a man if he gains the whole world, and loses his own soul? Or what will a man give in exchange of his soul" Matthew 16:24-26

In this life, for everything we do, there is a price to pay and a profit to receive. Some people pay the right price for the sake of the kingdom and later on in the future they will receive the winner's prize. Some others pay a negative price and equally receive a negative prize. There is an adage which goes thus "**No price no Prize**" Another goes thus "No pain no Gain». Some Christian are not willing to pay the price, this is the reason why they are being taken for granted by those who are not Christian. Anything that has a price, has a value. The price you pay for Christianity will determine the value you will obtain from it.

Most Christians talk piously about the cost of Christianity in terms of the unclean, injurious and sinful things they have "surrendered" But if they never get beyond that, they can still be referred to as common Christians. They talked about having given up bad things, but Paul the apostle said that for Christ's sake he surrendered the good things as well as the bad. "Whatever was to my profit, I now consider lost (Philippians 3:7a) He meant things to which he still had legal and moral right, things about which he could have said "these are mind and Christianity is not going to take them from me!" "I yield them; He said I give them because I have found that which is so much better." He was implying to the Phillipians. He had found "He" who was with the Father, Jesus Christ, the fountain from whom flows all wisdom, beauty, truth and immortality!

Paul knew something that many Christians still have to learn – the human heart is idolatrous and will worship anything it can possess. Therein lies the danger of good things. We have surrendered evil things, bad things, but we hold unto the good things and these we are prone to worship.

The Lord Jesus warned us about our selfishness in grasping and hanging on to our lives. He taught that if we make our life on earth so important and so all possessing that we cannot surrender it gladly to Him, we will lose it at last. He taught that plainly.

For Christians to be at peace with the Lord, they have to be hearers and doers of the word of God. The hand of God will always manifest for the benefit of humanity. But there is a special mark of ownership from the Lord, from such ones who listen to God's word, and put the word of God into action. It is for this reason that some people when they use the name of Jesus, it becomes a tower for safety; while others the same name is a stumbling block having no effect on them when they employ it on their life circumstances.

In life, some have gone through the great tribulation to be purged and cleansed as their final testing. They pay the ultimate price for their lives. Some suffered martyrdom, imprisonment, torture and even death for the sake of Christ. If we say we are Christians, there are some things which should not be mention among us. Yet because many do not want to take the responsibility, of knowing who they are, from the biblical stand they turn to oppose those who are practicing the truth and get themselves doing one atrocity or the other.

If you have been advised to stop your wrong doings, and you have refused to take the advice, take note that there is a price you will pay when your cup gets full. It is true some may be deceived by the fact that they have been doing such things, and nothing has happened by now, I will like to say what my pastor always says, "that your payment has not yet come because your cup is not yet full". When your cup gets full you will receive your prize and your crown for wrong doings.

Trying to look at the issue of paying the price in the academic domain, we will discover that students who went through their Doctorate program and finally defended it will tell you much about the price they paid before they obtained the Doctorate degree. They did not just sleep and relax and the Doctorate degree was taken and given to them. They will tell you that they paid the price of patience, hard work, and determination to see to it that the project gets to finalization. Some wake up and burn the mid night candle while their contemporaries slept. They paid the price dearly for their academic achievement and honour.

Some others, who went in for a competitive examination, and had a passed at the end, will tell you that they paid a price to get the success they are celebrating today. They did not fold their hands and go about making prophetic declaration doing nothing, or speaking in tongues that they will make it, but they took hard work as their watchword, and put it into action, after finished making their positive declaration.

They took the responsibility by getting to know the syllabuses to be used for that examination. And they did not end there. Some got themselves enrolled in private classes whereby teachers who were competent enough in their domain, enabled them have a deeper understanding of the subject matter. This made them successful when the results were published. They paid the price of hard work to get success. Their preparation for the examination enabled them to know the exact approach and materials to give out in order to be successful. The process of doing all these was not very comfortable but they followed the process to the end to get their objectives accomplished.

They have paid the price to be matriculated with the government as civil servants for the case of Cameroon, they will have the right to receive salary for a job done at the end of each month as long as they stay input to their jobs. This job came because of the sacrifice and determination they put in place to be successful at the end of the preparation period. Looking at this in line to our Christian life style, there is a price we equally have to pay. The apostle Paul in the book of Corinthians said *"You were bought at a price do not become slaves of men" 1Corinthian 7:23*

This scripture is letting us to be aware that we should not become slaves to alcohol, lies telling, cheating, envy, hatred, backbiting, etc. Sin is a reproach to any man, woman, family, nation, etc. Let us see an example of a man that God blessed with unusual anointing, but sin reduced him to zero. In life the price of righteousness is elevation and eternal life in the long run. And sin for a season most often, is not worth the price paid later on for it.

> *And it came to pass, when she pressed him daily with her words, urged him, so that his soul was vexed unto death; that he told her all his heart, and said unto her, there halt not come a razor upon my head; for I have been a Nazarite unto God from my mother's womb. If I be shaven then my strength will go from me, and I shall become weak, and be like any other man. And when Delilah saw that he had told her all his heart, she sent and called for the lord of the philistines, say, come up this once, for he halt showed me all his heart. Then the lords of the philistines came up unto her, and brought money in their hand. And she made him sleep upon her knees; and she called for a man, and she caused him to shave off the seven locks of his head; and she began to afflict him, and his strength went from him. Judges 16:16-19*

Samsom was playing with sin and at the end he was put in a total mess up. That was his prize for sin. One of the first thing sin does is to blind you. Sin always looks good at the beginning and suddenly, you are blind and will not know where you are going to; you will not have a sense of direction. They brought Samson down to Gaza and put him in the prison house to grind on a stone wheel. There he is blind bound and grinding day in and day out, week in and week out, month in and month out. Around and around he was maltreated. Samson has plenty of time to think now. He has plenty of time to "Listen to God! "What thundering pulsating words! If only He knows now that sin for a season is not worth the price, he is paying.

Each time you commit a sinful act, you do not only hurt yourself, but you hurt also those around you and those who love you most. Looking at Samson now, you would never recognize what has happened to God's son, a prophet of God, a ruler and a judge. Satan has reduced him to nothing. And this is satan's purpose for your life, to reduce you to nothing-zero. Perhaps you have watched people fall into this trap of Satan. For anyone in this tragic position, God still has a purpose for your life, a noble purpose. He does not want to leave you blind, bound, and grinding in the despair of defeat, humiliation and the inability to overcome. God wants you to hold your head up high in this world to be a winner, to be someone with the power of the life of Jesus-Christ.

Christian Suffering ends up in Glory if we do not Murmur or Complaint

God did not promise that we would never know sickness, face persecution or suffer hardships. On the contrary, we know that "all who live godly in Christ Jesus shall suffer persecution (2 Timothy 3:12) Jesus said in this world ye shall have tribulation.(John

16:33) We should know that our faith in God is going to be tested and tried, but God has promised us victory in every circumstance. Paul told the Corinthian "We are afflicted in every way, but not crushed; perplexed but not despairing, persecuted, but not forsaken; struck down, but not destroyed" 2Corinthians 4:8-9

When Christian suffered, they end up as good soldiers of the Lord always reflecting God's glory in their lives. When the Israelites were in Egypt, the Bible records that the more they were oppressed, the more they increase. Paul faced circumstances that were beyond his strength to endure, even to the point of despairing for his own life. He told the believers in Corinth.

> *"For we will not, brethren, have you ignorant of our trouble which came to us in Asia, that we were pressed out of life, but we had the sentence of death in ourselves, that we should not trust in ourselves but in God which raiseth the dead. Who delivered us from so great a death, and doth deliver, in whom we trust that he will yet deliver us" 2 Corinthians 1:8-10*

God is still in the business of delivering those faithful Christians who go through affliction. Paul did not moan, groan and complain about the hardships he suffered. He did not question God why He allowed these things to happen to him. He knew God was in control of his circumstances. Paul the apostle was not shaken by the hardship and suffering he went through. He did not put on a wrong attitude as some Christians usually put on when they are going through difficult situation.

Just like some will ask questions like why is God allowing troubles, hard breaks, famine and ugly happenings in their lives as Christians. Paul had a right attitude. He did not say I am weak and tired; neither did he say Satan had me this time. He was confident. He knew God was providing victory for Him in the present. He said, "He will deliver us" he knew that regardless of what he may face, God had already provided victory for him in the future. He said "*on Him we have set our hope that He will continue to deliver us*"

It was his knowledge about the provision of God's victory for him in the past, present and future that enabled Paul to face even death without fear. As he was preparing to die, he said "For I am now ready to be offered, and the time of my departure is at hand" (2 Timothy 4:6) he was not afraid of any circumstance Satan brought into his life-not even death-could defeat him, he said, "I was delivered from the lion's mouth. The Lord will rescue me from every-evil attack and will bring me safely to his heavenly kingdom"

How many times as a Christian, do you always find yourself doing some odd things, which are contrary to God's will, simply because you did not know. Paul's confidence came because of what he knew from the Bible about the mind of God for his life. He knew the promises of God for his life, and this made him confident. He had a revelation of who the Lord Jesus was to Him.

In life whether in the secular world or in your Christian faith ignorance of the law is not an excuse. So take responsibility in your walk with the Lord. If you do not know who you are, you will behave anyhow, and if you behave anyhow, you will be stripped of your honour. Knowledge of who you are will give you an advantage over the enemy. You will know how to and when to command what belongs to you and contest against the odd happenings in your life.

Knowledge of who you are as a Christian will make you live an upright life even if everybody around you is living a life contrary to God's standard. Meditate deeply now and let your imagination tell you how those in the King's palace do live and behave. Are they there to bring honour or disgrace to their Kingdom? Your answer will help you make a good decision from today to start serving God with sincerity of heart. You are the son and daughter of the King of Kings. What a great and valuable person you are, serve your King in reverence and in love. Is your God worth dying for, then take your responsibility and make things right with Him now for it's not too late. Do not

The Price of Self Denial

By faith Moses when he came to years, refused to be called the son of Pharaoh's daughter; choosing rather to suffer affliction with the people of God, than to enjoy the pleasures of sin for a season esteeming the reproach of Christ greater riches than the treasures in Egypt, for he had respect unto the recompense of the reward. By faith he forsook Egypt, not fearing the wrath of the king, for he endured, as seeing him who is invisible. Hebrews 11:24-27

The Lord approved Moses because he took the matter of self-denial at heart and put it in to practice, in his daily walk with God. The Biblical verses above make mention of the Man Moses. He was brought up in the king's palace but when he saw God's people suffering in truth, he decided to be a part with them. Jesus Christ said that, to be his follower, you **must deny yourself, carry your cross, and follow Him**. This is a threefold ministry in discipleship from the words of Jesus Christ that we are called to imitate and follow.

Denying the Self
Many who have paid this price see and find the world worth living. Anywhere they found themselves, whether there is no joy or peace, they can easily create one for themselves, because of the price of self-denial. We have been called out of self which is self-sufficiency, self-love, selfishness, self-seeking, self-gratification, self –righteousness, self-preservation, self-centeredness, self-knowledge, known as the flesh. (Matthew 10:39, 16:25, Mark 8:35, Luke 9:24, 17:33, John12:25)

All sins result from a pursuit of self –will rather than God's will. Self is prideful and arrogant. God would have us humble and meek; self-will wants us to be sovereign. God will want us to be dependent upon Him. We have been called out of all rebellion to God and must lay down all resistance and come back under His authority. Moses allowed himself to be inconvenienced (denied self) for God.

If you will do the same as Moses did, glory, honour, miracle will come to you. When we decide to seek God's will, we will be like a tree planted by the rivers of water that brings forth its fruit all-round the season.

Carrying the Cross
By nature most people are complacent and do not like change. When we yield to God, He wants to conform us to the image of His Son. (Romans 8:27, 14:17) The Holy Spirit works in us to meet that end – to grow and make us mature. The process is often very uncomfortable to the flesh (flesh carries a cross for transformation). There are peaks and valleys, trails and tribulation, and much self-denial. The flesh does not want to deny itself, the flesh does not want to love its enemies, the flesh does not want to carry the cross and yield to God's will-it prefers it own.

So if one is not following the spirit, spiritual growth becomes difficult, instead is the rebellion to God's will. The flesh wants to live in a way that satisfies self and not God. The main idea of carrying your cross is to portray that, if you are not being led by the spirit, then you are living apart from God's will in rebellion (opposed) to him. Then your purpose involves satisfying the flesh no matter how subtle it may seem. To reject the spirit is to reject Christ. 2Corinthians 1:22, 1John 4:13)

Many will seek the things of the flesh to satisfy self and love not the truth of God. The world says eat, drink and be merry for tomorrow we die. (Luke 12:19)Those who seek God die today, for they live in Christ. (Mark 8:35, Colossian 2:2,3:3)

Follow Christ
Following Christ means obeying the word of God each time it comes to you without arguing. A

follower obeys his master, and does not have any right to question His master on a point that the master has instructed Him on. As such if we say we are Christians, it means we are servants of God. Our obedience to instructions should not be questioned or argued if it's in line with the Bible. It is from our obedience to our master's instructions that our security, joy peace, love and happiness is guarantee.

Followers of Christ are to live like-minded with Him and as such are to be united with no division. 1Corinthians 1:10, 2Corinthians 13:11, Romans 12:16) God has to dwell in us richly. (Colossians 3:16) Believers are to edify, exhort, encourage, admonish, teach one another having been filled with the Holy Spirit. 1Thessalonian5:11, Hebrews3:13 Romans 15:6-7, 13-14, Colossians 3:16) Edifying is to teach and persuade each other in faith or in the truth and holiness. Exhort is to embolden, cheer and advice in strength of mind. Admonishing is to instruct and direct, or warn.

Moreover, to reprove with mildness, counsel against wrong practices, and as a servant of God abounding in all good work. Conforming ourselves to the teaching of Jesus Christ will bring us victory in this world, and will also cause us to reflect His glory which the world finds it difficult to understand.

CHAPTER THREE
SOME FALLEN CHRISTIAN VALUES IN THIS DISPENSATION OF GRACE

Here is a trustworthy saying, if we died with Him, we will also live with Him, if we endure, we will also reign with him, if we disown Him, He will also disown us, if we are faithless, he will remain faithful, for he cannot disown Himself. Keep reminding them of these things. Warm them before God against quarreling about words; it is of no value, and only ruins these who listen. (2Timothy 2:11-15)

When we take the mask off and take an honest look at the church today, we can see that sin has so infiltrated the church that it is difficult to distinguish some Christians from the world. The church is full of some religious people, who are professing Christ. However, their life style as to what they are professing to be is contrary to that. They are fulfilling the lust of the flesh without any regrets to their action.

Some others, who profess Christ, go to Church, dance, shout, and praise the Lord, but the minute they walk out of the door they begin to gossip, criticize and tear down the pastor or other members of the body of Christ.

There are some men and women who are bound by lust and are involved in adulterous relationships, yet see nothing wrong with it. They believe they can continue illicit relationships yet see nothing wrong with it. They are so-called Christians today who think nothing is wrong telling lies, stealing or cheating in their jobs. They take days off and call that they are sick, take supplies home from the office, take extra time at breaks, and extend their lunch hours.

There are some Christian business persons who think nothing of lying on their income, taxes and cheating their customers, purposely misrepresenting the facts, and becoming involved in questionable business deals with unbelievers. There are Christians who allow their hearts and minds to be filled with all sorts of evil imaginations and fantasies.

> *For the grace of God that brings salvation has appeared to all men. It teaches us to say "No" to ungodliness and worldly passions, and to live self-controlled upright and godly lives in this present age, while we wait for the blessed hope the glorious appearing of out great God and savior, Jesus Christ who gave Himself for us to redeem us from all wickedness and to purify for Himself a people that are his very own, eager to do what is good. Titus 2:11-14*

Some Christians watch movies filled with foul language, sex and violence, they tell dirty jokes on the job. All such things will not add to your life. They will only bring a minus or a negative sign in your life. Therefore if something will not bring profit into your life, it is needless to get yourself involve in such a thing. In many churches today worldliness is no longer condemned but encourage through doctrines that are being preached this cause Christians to set their affections on things of this world and teach them to seek material possession at the expense of the will of God. In many churches there are those who have an outward form of godliness but who are filled with hatred, bitterness, unforgiveness, pride, greed, jealousy and other ungodly attitudes.

Peter the Apostle, told believers, to "rid themselves of all malice, and all deceit, hypocrisy, envy, slander of every kind" (1 Peter2:1)

Taking your stand as a Christian involves so many things – imitating or following the footsteps of Christ, holding fast to your confession of the Lord Jesus as your Saviour and King, and being courageous that no man will come and take what belongs to you. Our model is Jesus Christ so we should have our focus on Him as the book of Hebrews clearly shows this truth.

"Let us keep our eyes fixed on Jesus, on whom our faith depends from the beginning to end. He did not give up because of the joy that was waiting for Him, He thought nothing of the disgrace of dying on the cross, and He is now seated at the right – hand side of God's throne." (Hebrews 12:2)

When we follow men who are not living according to God's standard, we will be derailing from the path of the Lord. This is because man has a way that seems right in his eyes. Man has limitation and at times seek self-glorification. But when we follow the Lord faithfully, He will see us through even in the darkest night. The Bible says God is an ever present help in times of trouble.

The First used of the Word Christian
The word Christian means Christ-like, this word was used to referred to the disciples when they were in Antioch.
> *"And when he had found him, he brought him unto Antioch. And it came to pass, that a whole year they assembled themselves with the church, and taught much people. And the disciples were called Christians first in Antioch. (Acts 11:26)*

They were teaching the people the word of God, and also observing and following the standard in the word of God. All what they were teaching, they were putting into practice. They were living exemplary lives before those they were preaching the word of God. What we observe in this dispensation of grace is that some who say are Christian cannot really differentiate between biblical and non-biblical principles. Many are ignorant of the word of God. They think the pastors are the only ones responsible to know the word of God. We are all called to know the mind of God from the Bible. Whether a pastor or not, it is your responsibility to have a good knowledge from the Bible. This will do you good and Christianity will not become a boring thing to you.

Instead of being, noisy, empty and carnal go in search of the mind of God from the Bible, and you will never regret it. Some even deceived themselves by living a wayward life, justifying themselves that once save, you are saved for life. This is a lie from the pit of hell. The Bible commands us to work our salvation with fear and tremble. (Philippians 2:12)

Do not be deceived; God cannot be mocked. A man will reap what he sows. (Galatians 6:7-9)

Following the Lord Jesus' examples, we should all live our lives in conformity with the Bible and we will never regret it. It takes a sincere decision for someone to make up his mind to live a life worthy of Jesus Christ.

Obeying Instruction as a Sign of Love
The issue of respecting and obeying instruction in relationship is an important sign of Love. Any relationship whereby instructions given by the boss is not followed, turns to be bound in frustration, abandonment, rebellion on the part of the follower who refuses to take instruction. The follower who refuses to obey most at times is exposed to menace from the enemy. At times, the gift of protection, which is his heritage, becomes difficult to attain because of the rebellion attitude. Relating this to our relationship with Christ is not different. Christ told Simon peter that if he loves Him let him feed his sheep. Meaning love goes along with obedience. Disobeying God's instruction and law will expose you to the menace of the enemy and will stripe you off your godly protection.

Some people have refused to follow Godly instruction, even when He speaks to them expressly in their conscience, or from the Bible. Jesus Christ our Saviour made mention of a true follower and a false follower. Meaning you can still be a church member, but you are not the sheep of Christ. If we decide to take up a godly Christian coat then let us follow the voice of the shepherd without complaining or criticizing.

"My sheep listen to my voice, I know them, and they follow me. I will give them eternal life, and they shall never perish; no one can snatch them out of my hand." (John 10:27-28)
"But they will never follow a stranger; in fact they will run away from him because they do not recognize a stranger's voice." (John 10:5)

God's voice comes to direct and teach a person when he is in confusion of what option to take as decision. It also comes to build us up, in the right path. Some Christians today have resorted to follow the voice of a stranger, which is leading them astray and to destruction. A stranger here refers to any man or woman who encourages you to go against God's will for your life. Be it a distant person or someone close to you. Be far from such a company, refuse to hear them when they call to give you instruction contrary to the will of God. You can do that in a courageous manner.

For example, a servant of God will hear God's instruction to do a particular assignment and the moment he shares it with those mature in faith than him, or to his spiritual fathers in the Lord, some will turn to discourage him or stop him from obeying God's voice.

Just like in the days of old, God gave instruction to his servants, some obey Him and some did not obey Him. Those who obey were approved by God and those who did not obey, had a disastrous end. My prayer for anyone reading this is that he or she should obey God with sincerity of heart. Some other Christian are being deceived with the fact that paying big amount of tithes and giving large sum of offering and yet continue in sin will make God to approved them and make them a candidate for heaven. It is not true. Others think the church is moving forwards because of their presence in the church. They go as far as saying that if they are not there the church will not continue existing. This is a false notion and if you are of such category repent and ask God for grace to serve Him as a faithful Christian.

Such people are only deceiving themselves. The Bible says we are workmanship created in Christ Jesus. We have to understand what Paul said in the epistle that "For it is God who is at work in you both to will and to do of His good pleasure." So then as we preach, give, sing, dance, and pray, in respect to God's word, we can then say, "Christ, you are the one doing all in my life".

Therefore, we need to walk with God. When we walk with God, He will approve of us as He did to some of our fathers of old. In the book of Genesis we read how Enoch walked with God and he did not see death. God took him away. Noah walked with God and he was saved from the flood. Daniel walked with God and he was saved from the lion's den. Joseph walked with God and his end was full of success and glory. He went through tough times but God delivered him from them all. Your case will not be different as you obey and walk with God. Meaning as a Christian, there are days when you will go through very difficult moment. Do not abandon, it will only be for a while. As it is often said, "when the storms are over, then come sunshine."

We should not be surprise of the many challenges, which will come, because of our devotion to God. At times challenges can come from anybody, but when they come, we should have a right attitude, be courageous and know our stand as children of God in this dispensation. There was a time in my life that people I respected and people I thought were people of integrity, went along marring my image by saying all sorts of evil things about me, which were not true. Reports later on came to me about such individuals, who were engaged in marring my image, I made up my mind to forgive and love them. I refuse to hate them it was not easy, but God gave me grace to forgive them. By nature, it is difficult to forgive, but the grace of God helps us to forgive even those who hurt us so deeply. Meaning forgiveness is possible by God's grace.

I also made up my mind not to be rule by people's opinion. This made me to give a dam to their claims. And I said everybody is entitled to his/her opinion. If we decide to walk with God with sincerity of heart, this will give us access to great testimonies, which will encourage others. For the devil might fight but God will give us a sure victory at the appointed time. A songwriter reminded us that it pays to serve the Lord. In that difficult moment we go through while serving the Lord, His grace will see us through. The Bible says "the arm of flesh will fail us and also that; we should have no confidence in the flesh."

Before Christ died, He gave a promise of going to plead the father for Him to send us the helper, who is the Holy Spirit. And that He will help us, guide us and stay with us forever. And I will ask the father, and he will give you another counselor to be with you forever- the spirit of truth. The world cannot accept him. However, you know him for he lives with you and will be in you. (John 14:16-17) Some Christians have no value for the Holy Spirit. Others do not believe that he is a personality in the Godhead. We need to rely on Him for without Him, the impossible cannot be made possible. The case of Mary in the Bible is an example of how the Holy Spirit can make the impossible, possible. He convicts us of our wrong doings. In another word, He enables us to serve the Lord with boldness and integrity.

Through Religion, Man will disannul the Word of God as in the Old Testament in the book of 1Kings 13:1-34 which narrates the story of two prophets. One heard God's instruction and decided to obey but deception came from another still a prophet, which derail him. At the end destruction came as a result of disobedience. But obedience in its totality is counted approve when the job assigned to do come to completion. In this story, God sent a prophet to Jeroboam king of Israel at the time concerning his sin of Idolatry (1 kings 13:7) the prophet was to deliver God's message and then return to Judah by a different way, not eating nor drinking in Israel. (1kings 13:8-9) The prophet in the course of obeying, another man, claiming to be from God changed God's word and deceived him (1kings13:15-18) the prophet then went to the false prophet's house ate and drank (1kings13:22-24)

God was very displeased and slew the prophet. Many will come in the name of the Lord and say, the Lord says…. We should be careful to follow God's word and direction. Others may test us be they Christians or not. (1 kings 13:26) When God speak we must obey regardless of what man says-even religious men. These religious men will say, oh my brother! When the damage is done (1kings 13:30)

Fellow brothers and sisters let us be responsible to God, by obeying his instruction without argument or secondary reasoning. Remember obedience has its rewards and disobedience has its own negative rewards. Let us do ourselves good and be wise not to join the company with those who are in the church and still refusing to depart from evil path.

Some Christians have decided to live carnal life style that is a life after the desires of the flesh. God's dealing with us is that we need to be transformed by the renewal of our mind. If not it becomes impossible to pleased God. In the book of Romans, it is written

"For to be carnal minded is death, but to be spiritually minded is life and peace. Because the carnal mind is enmity against God, for it not subjected to the law of God, neither indeed can it be. So then they that are in the flesh cannot please God" (Romans8:6-8)

The flesh will always ask a person to kill, tell lies, betray, gossip, mar people's image, fornicate, and shed innocent blood. If a person profess to be a Christian and is involved in all these, he should know that he is living in deception. Nevertheless, it is never too late, you can make up your mind now and stop any of such practices, and your life will never be the same again.

As Christians, we become conscious in the green light of His assured presence and go in that way, only stopping to consider what should be done when we see that the red light is there in case we go off the beam at any point. But to live in constant apprehension of the red light, is a dreadful distraction and frustration.

It is true many people at times say if what I'm doing is not good, God will have blocked me from carrying the act. The truth is that, God has given us a free will. He has presented good and bad to us and their consequences. It is up to us to choose. The Bible in the book of Philippians says,

"Wherefore, my beloved, as ye have always obeyed, not as in my presence only, but now much more in my absence, work out you salvation with fear and trembling. For it is God which worketh in you both to will and to do of His good pleasure. (Philippians 2:12-13)

Examine your life today. Are there some of those things mentioned above that you need to get rid of? If no, fine Ok continue steadfastly in the Lord. But if yes, make this bold declaration: "In the name of Jesus I reject malice, deceit, hypocrisy, envy and slander from operating in my life.

CHAPTER FOUR
THE GIANT AND HIS SOURCES OF STRENGTH

A giant is somebody large in size and stature who during a crisis can easily oppose his opponent. A giant is also a man with an extraordinary ability. A giant can be qualified as anything that stands on the way to oppose a person from getting to his objective. It takes courage to confront your giant and enter into your destiny. Courage kills fear. Until you take the potency of courage, you can never confront your giant.

> *"Goliath stood and shouted to the ranks of Israel, "why do you come out and line up for battle? Am I not a philistine, and are you not the servants of Saul? Choose a man and have him come down to me, if he is able to fight and kill me, we will become your subjects; but if I overcome him and kill him, you will become our subjects and serve us." (1Samuel 17:8-9)*

To every continent, nation, family and marriage there is a giant. For you to get to your throne you have to conquer the giant of your life. Giants can also be qualified as the breaks put on the way to stop people from attaining their life's objectives. When a giant wants to oppose a person, he is serious. That is he puts on the mechanism and the strategies on ground to see to it that the individual concerned becomes discouraged and defeated. A giant can stop its opponent from moving forward. Most at times, before a giant takes up its mission, he sits down and counts the cost before engaging. He takes all what he has to accomplish its task. Surprisingly some Christians do not bother to count the cost or pay the price it takes to overcome the giant along their path.

Giants on your way to your Inheritance
The Canaan land was a land flowing with milk and honey but on the way to the Canaan land there are giants. When you meet a giant on the way, he will not want to allow you to pass and get to your destination. They will launch a fight and prevent you from arriving at your destiny in life. The main aim or goal of the fight they usually launch is to bring about frustration, defeat, down cast, heartbreak and even despair. They have missions, which they are always determined to fulfill or accomplish. When they do that, do not be a coward by shying away from their attacks. The word of God says, when they come, you should contest with them, in other word engage a fight with them, and the God of heaven will give you victory over them.

> *"He is near that justifieth me; who will contend with me? Let us stand together: Who is mine adversary? Let him come near to me. Behold, the lord God will help me; who is he that shall condemn me? Lo, they all shall wax old as a garment; the moth shall eat them up.* (Isaiah 50:8-9)

The words of the Lord concerning our wellbeing are always words of victory and assurance. That is though the enemy is at work to see to it that our end should be without hope, the lord on the other side is saying they will all perish in a grave and moth shall eat them up. The Lord continues to encourage us that though the devil fights, our victory is maintained as long as we are obedient, courageous, respect and obey Him.

> *"When thou goest out to battle against thine enemy, seest horses, and chariots, and a people more than thou, be not afraid of them: for the Lord thy God is with thee, which brought thee up out of the land of Egypt. And it shall be, when ye are come nigh unto the battle, that the priest shall approach and speak unto the people."* (Deuteronomy 20:1-2)

The Lord is Omnipresence meaning ever presence and Omniscience He knows all. He is aware of the fact that when the enemy engages in a battle against an individual, a family, community and even a nation, he is serious and is looking forward for their destruction. The battle could end up in premature death of our visions, dreams, bright future and even physical death, if the Lord is not on our side.

In the past Christians will approach him with a cowardice attitude, which entails avoiding him. But as long as we do not face the giants of our life, we only postpone the battle and we will never inherit our throne. As such, courage and grace is required on our part to face the enemy and deal with him in order to inherit our throne.

The enemy has a policy of always intimidating his opponent. For us to face him in battle, we need grace to be courageous. Some people who were courageous to face the enemy, end up losing their life. It is not just a matter of you being courageous but grace is needed for you to be a winner in the battle. The enemy invests his time and energy before any confrontation. So when Christians want to engage him in a battle, they should put intact all the ammunition necessary. The scripture above says when he comes with horses, chariots and a people more than you. Horses and chariots for battle require money to be used for their preparation and cost. A people more than you, he goes about and mar our images, convinces people to fight against us. The Lord knows his canal weapons are sophisticated in battle and because of this, Himself the Lord will give us what it takes to defeat the enemy in battle. The Bible says;

> *But God hath chosen the foolish things of the world to shame the wise; and God chose the weak things of the world to shame the strong. He chose the lowly things of this world and the despised things- and the things that are not- to nullify the things that are so that no man may boast before Him.1Corinthians 1:27-28*

Relying on the Lord is the best thing any person can do to help himself go forward in life. God reigns in a royal palace as a king and He will never let the enemy of our life to destroy us. He will do everything to maintain our stability and our safety as we rest assure in His word and in His saving grace.

And all the people were at strife throughout all the tribes of Israel, saying, the king saved us out of the hand of our enemies, and he delivered us out of the hand of the philistines; and now he is fled out of the land for Absalom. 2Samuel 19:9

Putting this in our context, we will discover that God as our king will always save us and deliver us out of the hand of our enemy, when the enemies attack and seek to destroy our hopes, dreams, visions, etc. Having this in our mind, soul and spirit, we are called to be steadfast on the Lord. Relying on God does not mean challenges will not come. They will come but one thing we need to always keep in mind is that God will save and deliver us out of the hands of the enemies. These are great words of comfort and assurance that we should never neglect in our life no matter who we are or our position in life.

Most at times when people become great in life by having an achievement which they never thought of having, let's say by having a good job or say a good position in life.Some turn to put God far from their life and at times go about discouraging those who are placing their hopes and trust in God. We have to remember that the Bible we have is more than silver and gold. Therefore, we must cherish it with great care. It is written in the book of Revelation; *But that which ye have already, hold fast till I come. Revelation 2:25*

The word of God is advising us to hold fast till the end. This is because so many things can easily come across our way to cause us to give up. We should not easily give up in the battles of life. Whether we are winning or attacked by the enemy, or friends come to discourage us from the path of the Lord Almighty, we are encouraged to hold fast. Many things will come to test our faith, as we trust in the Lord Jesus Christ.

Qualifying Giants in our different Life's Experiences

> **The giant of ill health will come to disturb your healthy state.**
>
> *"Now He was teaching in one of the synagogues on the Sabbath. And behold, there was a woman who had a spirit of infirmity eighteen years and was bent over and could in no way raise herself up. But when Jesus saw her, He called her to Him and said to her, woman you are loosed from your infirmity." Luke 13:10-12*

Just as we have earlier given the definition of a giant as someone or something extra ordinary in stature which has the capacity to oppose its opponent. Ill health is a state of body, mind and spirit malfunctioning. The woman, who was crippled for eighteen years, had an encountered with Jesus and got her deliverance. The state of ill health had opposed her for eighteen years. That cripple state can be referred to as a giant of ill health. A giant does not care the number of years he will use just to see that you are destroy. Giants have ability to persevere. While on the other hand, some children of God easily give up in the battle of life. You have to stand your ground and oppose him by the grace of God. If not you will be in a constant state of ill health.

➢ The giant of poverty

The giant of poverty will come to keep you in a state of perpetual poverty. You cannot fold your hand doing nothing and go about making prophetic declaration like God will take control. The Bible says God will bless the work of our hands. As you engage in contenting against the giant of poverty, you must take action and get yourself doing one thing or the other, and then your victory over him will come, as you call and rely on God. If you are not aware of your position in the Lord, the giant will take an advantage over you and threatens you for the rest of your life on earth.

➢ The giant of pride

The giant of pride has a self-destructive effect. It will destroy its victim without remedy. As such you have to stand up and ask God to give you the grace to contest and overcome the spirit of pride in your life. You can pray like this, Lord give me grace to be humbled.

➢ The giant of stubbornness

The giant of stubbornness comes to oppose orders and advices given to you, which will help you to move forward. At times, the giant knows that respecting authorities will bring about your miracle or your break through. He will instill a stubborn will, which will have as target to stop the individual concern from receiving his miracle.

➢ The giant of fear and bondage

The giant of bondage puts you in a state of perpetual fear of the unknown. Fear of your fears, fear of what you are not supposed to be afraid of. Fear is the opposite of faith. Either you are faithful or you are fearful. It is a choice and your choice will determine how far you can go about, in achieving your God given objectives. You must stand up through prayer and faith in God to defeat the spirit of fear.

➤ The giant of sinful desire

The giant of sinful desire will hinder our spiritual growth. It was sinful desire that caused Cain to kill his brother Abel. Sinful desire caused Samson to reveal his secret to his enemies. It is written in the book of James1:5 *"then after desire has conceived, it gives birth to sin, and sin when it is full grown, gives birth to death."* Sin is a giant that opposes our spiritual life. Once you catch the disease of sin, it entangles your life like a spider web, chokes your spiritual life, and eventually brings spiritual death. You must throw off anything that causes you to sin. Then you can run the spiritual race without any hindrance. You must cut off all elements of sinful desires so that you can run the spiritual race.

Qualities of Giant Christians Ought to Know

1. His intimidating ability

"For forty days the philistine came forward every morning and every evening and took his stand." 1Samuel 17:16

Giant intimidates in a way that you finish by losing your confidence. Confidence is a very vital tool to use when in battle. A man, who is in battle and has no confidence, is already defeated before the start of the battle. So its better you do not engage in a battle when you seem to lose all your confidence. When the giant intimidates you, look up to God for courage and grace to overcome and have victory over him.

2. His size or stature

"A champion named Goliath, who was from Gath, came out of the philistine camp. He was over nine feet tall." 1 Samuel 17:4 Giant has size larger than the normal size, which makes them courageous. He sees his size as an advantage over his opponent, which of course is true. However, you as his opponent need to look up to God for Him to give you the grace and courage it takes to see you through. His large size is an opportunity for your weapon not to miss him when use on him.

3. His utterance ability

"Then the philistine said, "this day I defy the ranks of Israel! Give me a man and let us fight each other." On hearing the philistine words, Saul and all the Israelites were dismayed and terrified. 1 Samuel 17:10-11

The giant uses his utterance ability to instill fear in their lives. Just like he did in the days of old, he is still doing the same to Christians or individual even today. So brethren in Christ, beware of this trick so that you will not fall his victim. Today, he manifests this ability using let's say friends colleagues, classmate parents brothers etc. We should be vigilant not to be carried by his utterance ability. If he says a thing against you using any such medium, do not be gentle to respond. Respond by refusing his negative claims over your life

If not before you discover such things will begin to manifest in your life. For example let say you may be a young Christian sister, advance in age and you are not yet married, which of course you will get married by God's grace. Some church goers who know you, and do not have faith in God, will start to poison your mind with sayings like, don't you know that after thirty year, when a woman becomes pregnant, her pregnancy will be referred to as pregnancy at risk. You can respond by saying after thirty yours will be referred to as pregnancy at safety. The Bible says, *"From the days of John the Baptist until now, the kingdom of heaven has been forcefully advancing and forceful men lay hold of it." Matthew 11:12 NIV*

It is good to always have an answer to give for your favour when he says a thing against you. The Bible in the book of Job says, when men say there is a casting down, say there is a lifting up. Always say something when he attacks, do not say, "I am a quiet person in nature" be violent in your spirit against the wrongs of the enemy. With this style you will always be victorious and never be defeated in the battle of life. You should have a military mentality, and give no room for gentleman Christianity, if not you will spent your time and day murmuring or grumbling. And the Lord God will do just what he hears you say. *"So tell them, as surely as I live, declares the Lord, I will do to you the very thing I heard you say." Number 14:28*

Sometimes Christians are taught to give faith declaration, but many are not willing to confess what have been given to them for remedy of their problems. They find it too cheap and easy for a declaration to bring about manifestation. Believe it or not, will not change God's standard. It is one of those ways God brings things into manifestation.

4. His action ability
"*As he was talking with them, Goliath, the philistine champion from Gath, stepped out from his line and shouted his usual defiance, and David heard it. When the Israelites saw the man, they all ran from him in great fear." 1 Samuel 17:*23-24 A Giant always takes action to frighten his opponent. Goliath stepping out from his line and shouting is an action he demonstrated that made the Israelites to run away.

5. Knowledge of his Opponent
"*Goliath the giant stood and shouted to the ranks of Israel," "why do you come out and line up for battle? Am I not a philistine and are you not the servants of Saul? Choose a man and have him come down to me, if he is able to fight and kill me we will become your subject; but if I overcome him and kill him, you will become our subjects and serve us" 1 Samuel 17:8-9*

The giant knew the people he was going to confront in battle. He identified them as servants of Saul, which of course is true. How many times do Christians launch out to fight in a battle without knowing the enemy they are about to confront in question. Knowing the enemy means battle half won and will enable you to use the weapon of warfare appropriately. Without wasting them.

Facing a giant at any stage in life can be an overwhelming experience. Just look at David's battle with Goliath! God took an unsuspecting shepherd boy and helped him overcome his giant. By focusing on David of old and the ever-present God who is available to us even today, we can learn how to stand against our giants. In that one fateful day, David proved it to us why he was a man after God's heart. His victory reminds us that God can use anything in our hands if we have the right things in our heart!.

6. His persistent ability
We can see this in the book of Nehemiah chapter five. When Nehemiah decided to rebuild the walls of the temple. Samballant and Tobias came with discouragement, not once, not twice. But in all their tactics he answered them with just one word and after a while they gave up their vice.

CHAPTER FIVE
STRATEGIES TO ADOPT TO DEFEAT YOUR GIANTS

What is a Strategy?
A strategy can be defined as a plan that someone can use to achieve something. A strategy can also be the act of planning how to achieve something. In business term, for those who are in business and want the business to succeed, they draw down a plan to use to achieve business success; in this case we talk of business strategy. In war front, no matter how strong your enemy is, you can be able to defeat him if you have planned the strategies to use against him carefully. In a battlefield, your championship is determined by the strategies you have on ground.

Before any strategy is employed, knowledge of the enemy to be confronted is important. And in battle, you do not under estimate your enemy, if you do, he will take you unaware and defeat you. On the other hand, also you do not over estimate your enemy, if you do, you can get a break down and waste your weapons of warfare.

For the weapons of our warfare are not carnal, but mighty through God to the pulling down of strongholds. Casting down imaginations and every high thing that exalt

> *itself against the knowledge of God, and bringing into captivity every thought to the obedience of Christ. 2 Corinthians 10:4-5*

Be Prepared to Fight
A songwriter says "life on earth is a battle", that you must have a military mentality, you are called to always be ready, for battles. Christians are called to be alert at all times and not at sometimes. God is calling the church to prepare for battle. Satan is intensifying his attacks against God's people. To go out to battle without first activating and preparing your mind for the fight is like soldiers going out onto the battlefield without their weapons, unprepared to fight.

Before an army engages the enemy in battle, there must be a time of preparation. The weapons tanks and aircrafts are checked to see if they are in good condition. The commander in chief and other officers meet to plan their battle strategies. The soldiers go through all sorts of maneuvers simulating and acting out the strategies they are going to use during battle. The army is placed on alert. They are prepared physically and mentally to confront and fight the enemy until the war is won.

As you face the giants' attack on your mind, you must be prepared to fight and win the war. You must not be fearful or weak when the enemy takes the form of a giant to attack you. You must not be surprised, hide or feel sorry for yourself, whine, complain, or wonder why you are being attacked. We have been warned from the word of God about Satan's strategies. So you must be spiritually and mentally prepared to fight and withstand Satan and his forces until victory is yours.

Apostle Paul told the Corinthians "Be on your guard; stand firm in the faith; be men of courage; be strong. He told the Ephesians "finally be strong in the Lord and in his mighty power" (Ephesians 6:10) When you go out to battle, you must be strong and face the enemy not with your own strength but with the power of the most high God, that power that raise Jesus from dead. (Ephesian1:19-20) Therefore, no room for defeat. You must strengthen your mind for battle and prepared to fight knowing that He is sending you forth in His strength, in the power of a strong victorious mind. God has given His people the strength needed to fight and win in battle.

Some Strategies to use to overcome Giants

There are many strategies to use against a giant, depending on the size, nature of the giant, and the action he is taking to destroy your life or your God given assignment. Though there are many strategies to use in order to overcome and defeat your giants, we have carefully selected some strategies, which you can use against the giants who stand along your path to the fulfillment of your destiny. The following selected strategies will guarantee you victory as you study and put them into action, when you launch out to fight or confront a giant.

1. **FAITH**

    Now faith is the substance of things hoped for, the evidence of things not seen. For by it the elders obtained a good report. Through faith, we understand that the worlds were framed by the word of God, so that things, which are seen, were not made of things, which do appear. Hebrews 11:1-3

We can also define faith as a strong believe or trust in God. Or it is the belief that someone or something is good, right, and able to be trusted. The Bible definition says the evidence of things hope for is faith. Faith is the life wire of a Christian. For your faith to be at work, it must be coupled with prayers.

The woman who was diseased with the issue of blood for twelve years in the Bible heard about Jesus, and believed in her heart. She said in her heart "if I will only touch his garment, my story will not be the same." The Bible recorded that immediately she touched the Lord Jesus' garment, she was made whole. We have to understand here that she heard and made up her mind for the miracle and she obtained a good report. That was faith in action.

The disease of the issue of blood if we have to qualify it, was a giant in her life. The giant persisted until the day she rose up in faith and her story was no longer the same. She had faith that brought about her deliverance from what had threatened her for twelve years.

Your heart is the platform of faith. If you say you have faith, it will be expressed by your word and action. When you have faith, you will bring a good report from the land even if there are giants on the land. *By faith Abraham, when called to go to a place he would later receive as his inheritance, obeyed and went, even though he did not know where he was going. Hebrews 11:8*

Christians, let us have faith in God for if we have faith we will surmount every difficult situation on our path. The life of faith is not lonely. We have many examples to follow. The cloud of heroes and heroines of faith are fervently cheering us on to run the race well, to run the race to the end, and to receive the victor's crowns one by one. Abraham is cheering us to live by faith and Moses is cheering us to preserve to the end. Deborah is cheering us to rise to the challenge. King David is cheering us to be a good shepherd to the end.

2. GRACE

But by the grace of God I am what I am: and His grace which was bestowed upon me was not in vain; but I laboured more abundantly than they all: yet not I, but the grace of God which was in me. 1Corinthians 15:10

Grace is an approval or kindness in the Christian religion that is freely given by God to all human beings. The grace of God is the supernatural ability given to a person to accomplish a task, or a God given task. Grace is also divine favour. Grace is needed for somebody to overcome and defeat his giants. Grace also makes you to function without struggle.

You should never underestimate the grace of God in your life. If you take the grace of God for granted, you will be grounder. Just like some church goers today, use the grace of God as a licence to continue in their wrong doings. You did not know before now, let's just imagine so, that was the reason you were acting and doing things anyhow.

Now that you are aware of what the grace of God is all about, have respect for the grace, and stop using it as a licence to continue in wrong doing. An example of somebody who defeated a giant by the grace of God was David. Looking at Goliath the giant, it was obvious that he would defeat David in the battle if not of the grace of God that was with David. He had sophisticated weapons, he was well trained in battle, he had been a fighter for years, he could handle weapons of war because he had been using them for a long time.

David on the other hand was a shepherd boy, who was trained in keeping his father's sheep. When he faced Goliath, he did not count on his strength but he counted on the strength of the Lord. It is for this reason that when he was facing the giant, he said I am coming against you in the name of the Lord Almighty. David knew that for him to win the giant, he needed the God factor, which is grace. God does not save with sword and spear and with a shield. David won the battle because God's grace was with him. No doubt, my pastor will always define grace as God in the race. Meaning the G there stands for God and the remaining letters, which make up the word race. Putting the G and the word race together, will form the word grace. Embrace the grace of God and use it genuinely to accomplish your God given objectives. When God start using you to accomplish goals that your contemporary knew you could never accomplished, if not for the fact that God is with you, just be calm. If this happens to you, just put on the Apostle Paul's attitude who said *"Wherefore I was made a minister, according to the gift of the grace of God given unto me by the effectual working of His Power." Ephesians 3:7.*

3. DISCIPLINE

"No discipline seems pleasant at the time, but painful. Later on, however, it produces a harvest of righteousness and peace for those who have been trained by it." Hebrews 12:11 He who spares the rod hates his son, but he who loves him is careful to discipline him. Proverbs 13:24

Discipline is required to succeed in any area of life such as medicine, music, sport, science, education, military, and engineering. Most discipline teams become the champion in the game they venture in to. In the same way God disciplines His children for their growth and to become effective Bible teachers and powerful servants of God.

Discipline is the training, which produces obedience or self-control, often in the form of rules and punishments if these are broken. It could also be behaving in a controlled way. Discipline can be internal or external. External discipline is the one an association or an institution puts on you. Internal discipline is the one you impose in your life. Discipline is required to succeed in any area of life. No discipline seems pleasant at the time, but painful. Later on, however, it produces a harvest of righteousness and peace for those who have been trained by it." In the book of second Timothy, it is written *"study to show yourself approved unto God, a workman that needed not to be ashamed, rightly dividing the word of truth.* 2Timothy 2:5

For study to be effective and productive, discipline is needed. At times to get the winner's prize, one is called to be disciplined. Even the best world's football players have what they put on ground or what they use as a watchword which is discipline, for them to be world's champion. Remaining on the comfort zone will not help you. It will only destroy you.

Pride is a giant, which has a self-destructive effect. To conquer it, we must discipline ourselves either through fasting or through prayers asking the Lord to help us overcome such an attitude. Let us careful follow this remark made by a great Philosopher and try to gain understanding.

Seneca, one of the greatest of the ancient philosophers, said, "we should every night call ourselves to account. What infirmity have I mastered today? What passion opposed? What temptation resisted? What virtue acquired? And then he follows with this profound truth that "our vices will abate of themselves if they be brought every day to the shrift." If you cannot control your anger, learn to control your tongue, which like fire, is a good servant, but a hard master.

Let everybody who would not be shipwrecked on life's voyage cultivate this one great virtue, "self-control." There is nothing so important to a youth starting out in life such as a thoroughly trained and cultivated will; everything depends upon it. If he has it, he will succeed; if he does not have it he can fail. In training a person to acquire something in life, discipline is one the needed elements. *Train up a child in the way he should go and when he is old, he will not turn from it. Proverbs 22:6*

4. WISDOM

For wisdom is a defense, and money is a defense, but the excellency of knowledge is, that wisdom giveth life to them that have it. Ecclesiastic 7:12

Wisdom is the ability to use knowledge and experience to make good decision and judgments. My pastor Reverend Pastor Victor Obi defines wisdom as the wise are dominating. Some Christians are not interested to go out in search for wisdom. They are contented with what they already know and have, and are not interested to go for more. If by chance they happen to get a profound wisdom over a matter they know little about, they will find it difficult to accept the truth. At times, they will fight the source of information or the information itself. *Get wisdom, get understanding; do not forget my words or swerve from them. Do not forsake wisdom, and she will protect you; love her, and she will watch over you. Esteem her, and she will exalt you; embrace her, and she will honour you. She will set a garland of grace on your head and present you with a crown of splendor. Proverbs 4:5-9*

This quality will enable a person to get to his throne. You cannot get to the throne without overcoming the giant on your way to the throne. If not, in your promised land, you will have unrest and threats from the undefeated giants. Any giant you try to avoid instead of killing, you are only postponing the battle. Wisdom will enable you to get things done in the right way in order to conquer your giants who have decided to bring unrest and problems in your land, community, nation, and continent.

Most at times, some Christians turn to tolerate some giants who are not helpful in the fulfillment of their destiny. Any giant or evil you tolerate, today, will rise up to torment you in the future. So do not take side with the enemy. Wisdom is greater than weapons of war, wisdom gives you divine direction.

Have value for wisdom and it shall be well with your soul.

5. COURAGE

Be strong and of good courage, fear not nor be afraid of them: for the Lord thy God, He is that doth go with thee; he will not fail thee, nor forsake thee. In addition, Moses called unto Joshua, and said unto him in the sight of all Israel, be strong and of good courage, for thou must go with these people unto a land which the Lord halt sworn unto their fathers to give them and thou shalt cause them to inherit it. Deuteronomy 31:6-7

Courage is inspired boldness to overcome obstacles or confront obstacles. Courage is the ability to stand in the midst of fearful situation. Courage is not something that comes to your heart haphazardly, in moments of need or emergencies. Courage is not something that can be handed over to you through theoretical lessons either. Courage is a way of life. It is as much a habit as anything else. People tend to speak of courage only in terms of deeds.

For instance, they might speak of courage in the battlefield. Soldiers and police officers are supposed to show courage. On the other hand, they might refer to courage in the face of devastation. As Christians we need courage to carry along with, each breaking of a new day. Without courage, you will easily surrender before the outbreak of a spiritual or a physical war. That is to say, you have not yet fought and you are already defeated. Therefore, get possession of this quality, because the giants are always there to engage us in battle.

In the book of Joshua, we saw courage in action. This enables the leader through the help of God to draw up a plan to overcome the enemy's nation. Joshua sent two spies to go and survey the land of Jericho. They brought back reports that enable the leader to draw up plans on how to defeat the enemy nation. God granted them victory. The things the Lord demands from us is all for our welfare. He knew we would be faced with situations that can temper with our courage. As such He gives us a watchword in the face of any situation, that is be strong and courageous.

> *Be strong and courageous, because you will lead these people to inherit the land I swore to their ancestors to give them. Be strong and very courageous. Be careful to obey all the law my servant Moses gave you; do not turn from it to the right or to the left, that you may be successful wherever you go. Joshua 1:6-7*

6. KNOWLEDGE

My people are destroyed for lack of knowledge, because thou hast rejected knowledge, I will also reject thee, that thou shalt be no priest to me, seeing thou hast forgotten the law of thy God, I will also forget thy children. Hosea 4:6

Knowledge is the information and understanding that you have in your mind. It is often said that "If you are not informed, you will be deformed." To succeed in life you need the right information and knowledge. For you to do exploit, you need adequate knowledge. If you do not have knowledge, you will easily be deceived in this jungle of life. With flattery he will corrupt those who have violated the covenant, but the people who know their God will firmly resist him. Covenants are violated most at times because people do not have enough knowledge of their God.

Many people go to captivity because of lack of knowledge in their lives. You have to go for knowledge. If you do not want the enemy to chew you like bread go for knowledge. If you do not know who you are, you will cheapen yourself. And if you do not know who you are, you will not command the things you need. The giants take advantage most at times over Christians because many do not know who they are, and the abilities they have to overcome giants.

"Knowledge is the only guarantee of your entering into your inheritance. God has placed within each one of us, enough current that would give us light and make life meaningful and fulfilling. However, due to ignorance; many are still in poverty, disease and all kinds of oppressive hardship of the enemy. Whatever is not working in your life is not God's fault. It could either be your knowledge is inadequate. You need your own license of knowledge to walk in total freedom on this earth.

Knowledge is priceless. Nothing can be compare to it. No matter your position, your title, your experience, and what so ever you possess. In the absence of knowledge, darkness will prevail. The man who brought about computer technology did not have extra ordinary abilities. He had knowledge. He had an understanding on how to start computer technology. Knowledge is the key to freedom. It turns frustration to fulfillment, sweat to sweet. It is the power to dominion. Jesus puts so much value on it during his earthly ministry. At a point He indicated the lawyers for taking away the key of knowledge. He said this to them *"woe unto you, lawyers for ye have taken away the key of knowledge, ye enter not in yourself, and them that were entering in ye hindered. Luke 11:52*

7. JOY

The vine is dried up and the fig tree is withered; the pomegranate, the palm and the apple tree all the trees of the field are dried up. Surely, the joy of mankind is withered away. Joel 1:12

Joy is a feeling of great happiness. Joy is a needed factor to preserve the harvest and victory over the giants that stand to oppose you. Joy is a very important factor in this jungle of life; it is a weapon of strength. In life most often before the enemy attacks and destabilizes you, he start by tempering with your joy. Jeremiah understood the power of joy and he declared the word of comfort to the people. *Then he said unto them, go your way, eat the fat and drink the sweet, and send portions unto them for whom nothing is prepared, for this day is holy unto our Lord, neither be ye sorry; for the joy of the Lord is your strength. Nehemiah 8:1.*

We have to condition ourselves to be joyful in the Lord no matter the situation. Whether good or bad, whether in achievement or in despair we have to be joyful in the Lord. Being joyful will enhance a healthy state of mind and body on our side.

Although the fig tree shall not blossom, neither shall fruit be in the vines; the labour of the olive shall fail, and the fields shall yield no meat; flock shall be cut off from the fold, and there shall be no herd in the stalls; yet I will rejoice in the Lord, I will joy in the God of my salvation. Habakkuk 3:17-18

8. PERSISTENCY

"Saying there was in a certain city a judge who did not fear Godnor man. Now there was a widow in that city; and she came to him, saying get justice for me from my adversary. And he will not for a while; but afterward he said within himself though I do not fear God nor regard man yet because this widow troubles me I will avenge her, lest by her continual coming she weary me. Luke 18:2-5.

Persistency is the characteristics of all men who have accomplished great things. They may be lacking in some domains, have weaknesses or eccentricities, but the quality of persistence was never absent or lacking in a successful man. Whatever the opposition he meets, or discouragement he encounters, he is always persistent. Obstacles cannot discourage him, labour cannot weary him. He will persist, no matter what comes or what goes; it is a part of his nature. Persistency always gives confidence. Everybody believes in the man who persists. He may meet misfortunes, sorrows, and reverse, but everybody believes that he will ultimately triumph because he knows there is nothing that can keep him down. Even the man with small ability will often succeed if he has the quality of persistence, where the genius without persistence would fail.

9. OBEDIENCE

By whom we have grace and apostleship, for obedience to the faith among all nations, for His name: Among whom are ye also the called of Jesus Christ (Romans 1:5-6) Obedience is doing what one has been instructed to do. In talking to children, you may say, "will you please obey me and do what you are told to do?

What we mean is please carry out my instructions. Obedience carries with it the thought of subordination or recognition of authority and wisdom. It is an attitude of hearing and putting into action instruction. Obedience is an attitude of the mind towards a higher authority. As Christians, our higher authority is God Himself. The Lord said in *John 14:15 if ye love me keep my commandments.* Obedience also deals with the individual's attitude towards God. Anyone who loves God will keep His commandment.

To conclude, these are some strategies that when carefully employed against the giants, your success will be guarantee and the victory will be yours. A songwriter says life is a battle. For you to be a winner in this battle of life apply these points and the victor's crown will be your portion in this life and you will walk with a courageous heart after the Lord on a daily base. The freedom fighters of old, warriors, who stood their grounds and defeated their enemies, had some of these qualities. Those who got themselves engaged in battles to fight against the odd happenings in their nation, family, tribe, etc. did not lack some of these qualities.

CHAPTER SIX
REWARDS FOR ROYALTY

For I know the thoughts that I think towards you, saith the Lord, thoughts of peace, and not of evil, to give you an expected end. Jeremiah 29:11

Reclaiming Christian's Royalty
Royal is an adjective, which describes a person or persons belonging or connected to a king or a queen or a member of their family. God our father is the King and we his children are princes and princesses. In every kingdom, the children of the king are entitled to some privileges. However if your father is a king and you are not aware of your father's status and right, you will suffer. That is what is happening to many Christians in this dispensation of grace. *"What I am saying is that as long as the heir is a child, he is no different from a slave, although he owns the estate." Galatians 4:1*

Who is a Child?
A child in the context above does not only refer to a kid. A grown up who has refused to take responsibility to seek God's will, and who does not know his right can also be likened as a kid. For if you do not know what God is saying you will not be able to walk according to the Biblical standard. God has

given us everything that pertains to life and godliness but if you do not make good use of it, nobody is to be held responsible if not yourself. The Bible says my people are destroyed for lack of knowledge not because of the devil. Therefore, if we want to live a good life then we should go to the Bible and see what God has for us and our life will never be the same.

Some Christian today are in a state of confusion and have refused to take responsibility in finding out God's mind for their life from the word of God. This state has given the enemy right over them; by manipulating them, as he wants. However, if Christians will discover themselves today, their life will be colourful and meaningful in this dispensation of grace.

The Place of Thought in Reclaiming Royalty
Thought of reclaiming the Christian royalty because you are a product of what you think. Thoughts have a great deal to do with the destiny of any man, clan, tribe, family, nation and continent, etc. Thinking is one of the activities of the mind. What you think of yourself, your circumstances or your giants, will ultimately become manifest. *"For as he thinketh in his heart, so is he: Eat and drink, saith he to thee; but his heart is not with thee." Proverbs23:7.*

Destructive, negative and bad thoughts are degrading as creative positive and good thoughts are uplifting. If you do not think of becoming somebody important and influential, you cannot become. If you think of failure, before you discover, you will see it manifest in your life. Every negative thought you allow to have a grip in your life, blocks you from entering into your inheritance in Christ Jesus.

Thoughts are factors, which help you to take action or decision.

Before a man engages in insulting or marring another man's image, thoughts projected first on the inside of such a person before its manifestation. And not just any type of thought. Negative thoughts produce negative effect, and positive thoughts produce positive effect. It is up to us to make a choice if we wish to live peaceful with all men. So it is important to guard the thoughts of your mind. If not they can lead you astray if the thoughts are negatives.

"But those things which proceed out of the mouth come from the heart, and they defile a man. For out of the heart proceed evil thoughts, murders, adulteries, fornications, thefts false witness, and blasphemies. These are the things which defile a man, but to eat with unwashed hand does not defile a man."

Our thoughts and words are weighed before God. Blind Batimaeus heard about Jesus, this implies after he heard, a thought was projected into his mind that made him to take action and decision. The same impact that positive words have in decision and action taking, is the same way negative words came produce destructive effects. So you should be careful about the things you hear and say from your environment.

Blind Batimaeus got up and shouted out for his deliverance. People around told him to stop shouting, but still the more he shouted aloud. The people around wanted to impose their decision and opinion on him. However, he did not allow their opinion to influence his decision. At the end, he obtained his miracle from the Lord Jesus Christ.

Everything we do originate from the thought. Therefore, think well and it shall be well with you. Think evil and before you discover things will start working against you. The choice is yours. In the spiritual realm, any thought that has grip on your mind is regarded accomplished. It will need then time to manifest in the physical. Most at times before your mouth utters a word, the issue must have been well settled in the mind. This is faith principle. Thoughts will either make you or break you.

The reason why Christians are not living Christianity as a lifestyle is because they speak positive about a situation in the outside, but are negative in the inside. Their words do not tight to their thoughts. This is hypocrisy as the Bible qualifies such an attitude. Your thought and your confession must be in agreement before you can have a manifestation. God Himself do think. As such if we are the children of God, we have to get into this business of thinking which will cause you to take action for your well-being.

"The Lord of Host halt sworn, saying, surely as I have thought, so shall it come to pass; and as I have purposed, so shall it stand." Isaiah14:24

God do think and his thoughts are pure and positive. So if we must desire to reflect God's glory, we must get ourselves involve in positive thinking. By doing this we will see ourselves reclaiming our Christian royalty. *Search me, O God, and know my heart, try me and know my thoughts. Psalms 139:23*

The Psalmist from the scripture above is pleading God to search Him. Here we understand that if God searches and sees that your thoughts are right before Him He will bring into effect the good thoughts into manifestation and vice versa. Your healing, your breakthrough, your deliverance, your promotion, your peace of mind will be made manifest if your thought is in conformity with the word of God. He searches and sees the desires and expectation, for Him to bring to pass the expectation. He does not take pleasure in evil thought. Evil thoughts are destructive so it is not the will of God for us to experience destruction.

> *He takes pleasure in our prosperity. Let them shout for joy, and be glad, that favor my righteous cause, yea let them say continually, let the Lord be magnified, which halt pleasure in the prosperity of His servant. Psalms 35:27*

God takes pleasure in our prosperity. Therefore, we should desire to prosper in all domains in life. It could be in the domain of health, academics, ministry, finance etc many people have a false notion about God. Some think God is a terrible Father and that He can just destroy them when they make an error. It is a false notion.

Our God is a good God. The scripture above makes us understand that God takes pleasure when we prosper. So think prosperity and you shall prosper, think of being healthy and you will see its manifestation in Jesus' Name. On the other hand when you think of failure, before you discover it will start manifesting in to your life. You can make up your mind to start nursing positive thought concerning yourself and concerning those around you.

> "*Finally brethren, whatsoever things are true, whatsoever things are honest, whatsoever things are just, whatsoever things are pure, whatsoever things are lovely, whatsoever things are of good report, if there be any virtue, and if there be any praise think on these things"* Philippians 4:8

The positive must be the basis of your thoughts if you wish to see good change in your nation, city, town etc and for the supernatural to be at your command.

The Slogan in God's Kingdom

Every kingdom has a slogan. The kingdom of God is based upon righteousness. Its foundation is based on Holiness.

> "*But unto the son he saith thy throne O God, is for ever and ever, a scepter of righteousness is the scepter of thy kingdom. Thou hast loved righteousness, and hated iniquity, therefore God halt anointed thee with the oil of gladness above thy fellow.*" Hebrew 1:8-9

A scepter is a symbol of royal power or authority. God's kingdom is a righteous kingdom; therefore you as a Christian should be imitators of God your Father. You should obey and follow God's instruction because all what He tells you is for your own good.

Righteousness is a weapon of offence and defence. You should take responsibility to live a righteous live in your words, action and whatsoever you do. This will make your life beautiful and also make the world you are living in beautiful and worth living. To them who by patient continuous in well doing seek for glory, honour immortality and eternal life. That is just who you are as you make up your mind to please God. Endeavor to maintain this code of conduct as a Christian. In this dispensation, when truth is not easily accepted, practiced, taught or heeded, he that lives a righteous life style becomes a prey for those religious ones. As a Christian, no matter your denomination, your country or your continent, go for the truth and you will never regret it. You will be happy, as God will manifest His glory in your life, for the world to see the light of God in you and so glorify and honour His name.

Christian Royalty and Some Duties

God's desire for His Children is for them to reignand have dominion. However, we realize that at times Christians are being dominated by some evil forces found in the nature. "Before you reign, you must be trained" God has many ways to train us in order for us to take our office for the purpose of advancing His kingdom here on earth. We realize that even in the secular institutions, some who started a particular training and end up not finishing their course will not receive the prize or the award of the diploma or certificate they went in for. It could be that the training course was too stressful or demanding, and since they could not build qualities of resistance, to meet up with the training demands, they turned and gave up. For some who will wish to attempt the training and discover that the training will temper with their comfort, such ones will not always dare for such training. These are those who have chosen to remain in their comfort zone.

However, as world changers, comfort zone is not always a priority most at times because there are battles and victories to be won. Some others, who think the training will temper with their pride, will not just identify themselves in line with such training. But then they need to be trained in order to function in their office. Those who will be recruited and given a post in line to the training course offered, will be those who through determination and perseverance went through the training successfully.

God's purpose of taking us through some training in life, is to make us the envy of the nation and to reflect his glory in our life. In a kingdom, the king always gives out attributes a person needs to possess in order to serve his people. Moreover, the king will not just appoint any person to a particular office. For you to be appointed, you must be approved as a trustworthy servant. He will carefully seek for those who understand the kingdom's principles and are willing to be guided by the principles. He will choose those who are willing to die or sacrifice their pleasure, time, pride, self for the advancement and prosperity of the kingdom. This is because, anyone who has not dealt with the attitude of self-pride, or self-centeredness, will not seek the welfare of the kingdom. But rather his own welfare at the detriment of others.

Just like some good qualities, some earthly kings will seek those with such qualities before they dare appoint them to an office to serve their people, so also our God is a God of standard. He seeks such standard qualities from His servants after they must have gone through some training, for them to serve His people with love, equity and justice. So if you wish to serve God's people, endeavor to reach out for the best that God is asking from his servants as the Bible prescribes.

Things That Will Happen to You for Maintaining the Kingdom Royalty

- You will be a priest and a holy nation to be above all people. (Exodus 19:6, Revelation 20:6)
- You will be a people dedicated to God alone and you will serve Him as Priests.
- You will reign over many nations (Deuteronomy 15:6)
- God will become an enemy to your enemy (Exodus 23:22)
- You will have right to the tree of life (Revelation 22:14)
- God will bless you with favour and shield (Psalms 5:12)

Things You will get for Reclaiming the Kingdom Royalty

- You will have a royal crown or royal diadem (Esther 5:8, Esther 1:11, 2:17 Isaiah 62:3)
- You will have a royal Majesty (1Chronicles 29:25)
- You will get a royal bounty (1Chronicles 29:23)
- You will have a royal command. A command that once you pronounce or make a declaration, it cannot be distorted. (Esther 1:19)
- You will have a royal house.
- You will have a royal dignity

- You will have a royal estate (Esther 1:19)
- You will have a royal apparel (5:8)
- You will have a royal throne
- You will have a royal seed. (2Chronicles 25:25, Jeremiah 41:1)
- You will have a royal seal (2Kings21:8)
- You will have a royal robe (2 Kings 22:10)
- You will be of a royal standard (2Samuel 14:26)

Make this Bold Declaration

- I obtained kindness from the Almighty King of the Universe to execute my function faithfully in Jesus' name. Amen
- No man or woman will take my place in Jesus' name. Amen.
- May I be preferred more than my contestant in Jesus' name amen.
- Whatever negative decree that was made against my life, I send it back to sender in Jesus' name Amen.

CHAPTER SEVEN
MILK AND HONEY

Milk is the liquid produced by cows, goats and sheep used by human, as a drink, or for making butter or cheese. Milk is also the white liquid produced by women and other female mammals as food for their young ones. "Milk and Honey" originate in the Hebrew Bible from which God described the country lying between the Mediterrean Sea and the Jordan River, named, Canaan. It is first describe as "a good and spacious land, a land flowing with milk and honey" which God commissioned Moses to lead the Israelites into the Land.

"Milk and Honey" is a metaphor meaning all good things – God's blessings; and the promised land being the land of extraordinary fertility. The phrase "flowing with milk and honey" is understood to be a description of the land's richness; hence it is currently used to express the abundance of pure means of enjoyment.

Speaking of the Lord's kingdom; milk represents spiritual goods; that which is happy, pleasant, and delightful.

> *Thus wast thou adorned with gold and silver; and thy garments were of fine linen, silk, and broidered work. Thou didst eat fine flour and honey and oil; so thou becamest beautiful*

very exceedingly, and thou didst prosper even unto a kingdom. With fine flour and oil and honey I fed thee; but thou didst set it before them for an odour of rest (Ezekiel 16:13,19)

Speaking of Jerusalem, by which is meant the spiritual church, this quality has been used to describe it as it used to be in the ancient time and as it will become in the future. Her being adorned with gold and silver represents celestial spiritual good and truth; also her garments of fine linen, silk, and broidered work stands for truths.

Honey

Honey is a sweet sticky yellow substance made by bees and used as food. Honey symbolizes delight. This is because anything sweet in the natural world correspond to what is delightful and pleasant. Honey symbolizes what is delightful, this evident from the word of God can be seen in the book of Isaiah 7:14,15 A virgin shall conceive and bear a son and shall call His name Immanuel (God with us). Butter and honey shall He eat, that He may know to refuse the evil and choose the good (Isaiah7:14,15) In the same light it shall come to pass for the multitude of milk that they shall yield, he shall eat butter; and butter and honey shall everyone eat that is left in the midst of the land (Isaiah7:22) In the same, Judah and the land of Israel were thy traders, in wheat of Minnith, and pannag, and honey, and oil and balm (Ezekiel 27:17)

Honey here also denotes the pleasantness and delight from the affections of knowing and learning celestial and spiritual goods and truths.

Some Biblical cited cases concerning Honey

To Moses:-Thou makest him ride on the high places of the earth, and he eats the produce of the fields. He maketh him suck honey out of the rock, and oil out of the flint of the rock (Deuteronomy32:13); it also refers to the ancient spiritual Church. To suck honey out of the rock, stands for delight of truths and memory –knowledge.

To David:-I feed them with fat of wheat, and with honey out of the rock I sate them (Psalms81:16); to sate with honey out of the rock means to fill with delight from the truths of faith.

Jehovah bringeth me unto a good land, a land of rivers of water, of fountains and of deeps that go out from the valley, and from the mountain; a land of wheat and barley, and of vine and of fig and pomegranate; a land of olive oil and honey (Deuteronomy 8:7,8)

The land of Canaan was a land flowing with milk and honey (Number 13:27, 14:8 Deuteronomy 26:9, 27:3, Jeremiah 11:5, 32:22, Ezekiel 20:6) In the internal sense of these passages the land of Canaan is meant, to give allusion, to the Lord's kingdom; flowing with milk, denotes an abundance of celestial, spiritual thing including happiness and delights.

In David:-The judgments of Jehovah are truth and righteous more to be desired than gold and much fine gold, sweeter also than honey and the dropping of the honeycombs (psalms19:9, 10)

The judgments of Jehovah represents divine truth; sweeter than honey and dropping of the honeycombs. *"sweet are thy words to my palate, sweeter than honey to my mouth" (psalms 119:103)*; A similar meaning can be seen in the manna that

Jacob's posterity had for bread in the wilderness, this description was also referred to Moses "the manna was like coriander seed, white and the taste of it was like a cake kneaded with honey"(Exodus 16:31)

Manna signified the Divine truth that descends through heaven, from the Lord, it consequently signified the Lord Himself as the Divine Human as He teaches in (John 6:51, 58); for it is the Lord, from which all Divine truth comes, yea, of which all Divine truth flow; and this being so, the manna is described in respect to delight and pleasantness by the taste. The taste denotes the delight of good and the pleasantness of truth.

The delight of Divine truth in respect to the external sense is also described and referred to honey. In Ezekiel, 3:3 He said unto me, son of man, feed thy belly and fill thy bowels with this roll that I give thee. And when I ate it, it was in my mouth as honey for sweetness.

And John:-

> *The angel said unto me, Take the little book and eat it up; and it shall make thy belly bitter, but it shall be in thy mouth sweet as honey. So I took the little book out of the angel's hand and ate it up; and it was in my mouth sweet as honey; but when I had eaten it my belly was made bitter. Then he said unto me, thou must prophesy again over many people and nations and tongues and kings (Revelation 10:9-11)*

The roll in Ezekiel, and the little book in John, denotes truth. In the external form this appears delightful, and is signified by the taste being sweet as honey; for divine truth just like the word is delightful in the external form or in the literal sense because this admits of being unfolded by interpretations in everyone's favour. But it is not so in the internal sense, which therefore signifies the bitter taste; for this sense discloses man's interiors.

The reason why the external sense is delightful is because the things in it can be unfolded favourably; for they are general truths, and general truths are susceptible. It is delightful also because it is natural, and what is spiritual conceals itself within. Moreover, it must be delightful in order that man may receive it, be introduced into it, and not be deterred at the very sight.

From all this we can now see that by honey we mean the delight that is from good and truth, or from the affection of them.

Virtues of Milk and Honey
- Milk and honey have medicinal values.
- Honey has preservation ability.
- Honey has an embalming virtue.
- Honey as a gift given to someone, signifies a love portion.
- Honey opens the flesh and knits together the bones and gathers together all parts of the body.
- Milk and honey as symbols of fertility appears in most ancient writings.
- Honey signifies riches, glory and gladness.

The Canaan Land
> *"And the Lord spake unto Moses and unto Aaron, say, how long shall I bear with this evil congregation, which murmur against me?*

I have heard the murmurings of the Children of Israel, which they murmur against me."
Number 14:26-27

God has promised to give the children of Israel the Land of Canaan, but not without many battles. Innumerable enemies had to be conquered before they could enter the promised Land. With so great a destiny as the promised land, why delay? What was the aim of the aimless wandering? God has to first prepare the new generation for the promised inheritance. Time was needed for the older generation of slaves who had complained and rebelled, to die in the wilderness.

In this we can say God has a way of dealing with his people today. There are times in the Christian's life when the years pass, opportunities come and go, and life hastens on towards its close, but so little progress seems to be made in transforming our character, so little eternal work accomplished. Are the wasted years evidence that much in us of old nature is not yet buried?

The fruitless years of the past need not be in vain. We should recognize our "desert experiences" as means of dying to unbelief and as the divine design to prepare us for spiritual service. *"We came unto the land wither thou senteth us, and surely it floweth with milk and honey. We be not able to go up against the people; for they are stronger than we"* *(Numbers13:27,31)*

Some people usually asked the question like "why did God lead the Israelites to a land (Egypt) where He knew they would become slaves?" He did it to protect them! He knew that serious wars would break out in Canaan during the time they were in

Egypt. Being weak, they would have been destroyed if they had not stayed.

The Lord would have you learn from the Children of Israel. Maybe He is leading you to a job or housing in an unlikely place to protect you! You cannot imagine what the enemy may be plotting, but God knows. He needs to put you somewhere else for a time to strengthen you. Do not worry. When the time is right, He will lead you back to Canaan. You should be assured that God would do anything He has to protect you. The Psalmist confirmed this

> *"For this cause, everyone who is godly shall pray to you in a time when you may be found; surely in a flood of great waters. They shall not come near him. You are my hiding place; you shall preserve me from trouble; you shall surround me with songs of deliverance. (Psalms 32:6-7)*

Twelve leaders of Israel were chosen to explore the land of Canaan (numbers 13:3, 17-20) So the men went North and explored the land and came to Hebron (Numbers 13:21-22) But ten (10) of the spies failed to believe in God's promise. They could see only the high wall and the giants. Not knowing that our eyes are supposed to be set on the big God who will remove the big obstacles on our path.

Joshua and Caleb spoke in faith and knew God will be with them in the battle. Grace to over throw the giants. (Number 14:9) The people refused to trust God and exercise faith in Him. They decided to portray the enemy as being too powerful to be defeated before their attempt to act upon the word of God.

Depending upon human reasoning and physical strength before committing oneself to the Lord's work reveals a lack of faith in God's ability to fulfill His promise. Many people become frightened at the giants of difficulties. Even the weakest Christian who will trust in God's strength can accomplish what the Lord wants him to do. (Philippians 4:13) Without faith we cannot please God. Faith is the surest weapon we ought to use, to fight against the giants trying to stop us on our way towards achieving our God giving destiny.

> *"But I will not drive them in a single year, because the land would become desolate and the wild animal will become numerous for you, little by little I will drive them out before you, until you have increase enough to take possession of the land. I will establish your borders from the sea of Philistines and from the desert to the river. I will hand over to you the people who live in the land and you will drive out them before you." Exodus 23:29-31*

The journey of the old Testament Israelites from Egypt to the promised land can be likened to the experiences of the new testament Christians in their pilgrimage to Spiritual rest and maturity. Many of us have gone through comparable, long wilderness journeys in our quest for peace and victory, though at times we may not realize it. God's chosen people wander from Egypt to the outskirt of the promise land for forty years, but their lack of faith prevented them from entering the promised Land.

Of the twelve spies sent to survey and check the land, only Caleb and Joshua said "let's go in; we can do it." This was courage in demonstration and action. Stop here for a while and make this declaration. Make this declaration, any situation, thing, or circumstance that has been tormenting and frightening me, I receive courage and grace from God Almighty to confront and overcome it in Jesus Name.

Two people can face the same situation, and one becomes a winner while the other becomes a loser. It is a matter of choice for you to be either a winner or a loser. Out of the twelve sent to survey the land, ten (10) had a bad report while two of them came with a good report. The two understood that faith in God says all is well, even if the situation appears deplorable. It does not matter the population following the wrong direction away from God's purpose and will. God will always save the hand full though seem to be the minority that follow and obey his instruction. Apostle Paul said "God is not a respecter of person".

Always have this in mind that in the promise land, battles, frustrations, temptations and tensions of every day's life do not suddenly end. There are enemies in this new found land that must be dealt with. However, you are more than conquerors in this new land. In the book of Exodus, God promised the children of Israel that He will drive the enemies out of their land little by little but He also speaks of a future day when they will fight with authority and will drive the enemy away from their land. Meaning that, during this time you will take your God given authority to fight and drive the enemy. Exodus 23:29-31

We can see that there are two stages of Canaan living. The first stage, we are containers who merely watch God in action. While in the second stage of Canaan living, we have matured into full persons who act on God's behalf as His ambassadors. Would you love to be a spectator or God's agent in action. Are you waiting for God to take care of all the enemies and mountains in your life while you just watch, or are you handling life as a whole person?

The verses from Exodus indicate that we should anticipate the day when we finally "become" fruitful and take possession of the land. At that point God will deliver the inhabitants of the land into our hand, but we will drive the enemy out before us. Paul wrote to the Galatians that a son will take charge of some affairs only when he grows up to maturity. Galatians 4:1-4 To take charge does not mean to rely on your effort that is self-effort. No amount of determination, praying or fighting will give you victory if not of God's grace. *So then it is not of him who wills nor of him who runs, but of God who shows mercy. Romans 9:16.*

Bibliography

1. D. Conway Stone, 1995, *Follow Your Dreams,* Pinnacle of Grace Publishing.

2. D. K. Olukoya, 2005, *Paying Evil Tithes,*

3. David .O. Oyedepo, *Releasing the Supernatural: An adventure into the Spirit World.*

4. E.M Bounds, *Power Through Prayer.*

5. Francois Yanze, 2011, *Les Opportunities de la Vie,*

6. Gerald I. Nierenberg, and al, 1971 *How to Read a Person like a Book.*

7. Itambon Victor Obi, 2011, *Divine Strategies for Exploits in Life,* Rhema Publications Yaounde, Cameroon.

8. Itambon Victor Obi, 2011, *Access to the Voice Of God,* Rhema Publications Yaounde, Cameroon.

9. Itambon Victor Obi, 2008, *When the heavens are Opened.* Rhema Publishing House Yaounde.

10. Mary Charles Anyanwu, 1993, *Discovering Yourself in God and for God.*

11. Mike Murdock, *31 reasons people do not Receive their Financial Harvest.*

12. Mike Ubi, 2003, *Ultimate Security Daily Word*, J.V.C Publication Nigeria.

13. Oral Roberts, Don't Give Up! JESUS will give you that MIRACLE you need.

14. Orison Sweet Marden, *How to Succeed, Divine Favour* Christian Publishing Benin City.

15. Rod Parsley, 1999, *Adventuring with CHRIST.*

16. Sonffo T.G, *Comment devenir tout ce pourquoi vous avez été crée*, 2010 Harvesting Publishing House Yaounde-Cameroon.

17. Watchman nee, 1999, *The Release of the Spirit.*

18. Zacharias Tanee Fomum, 1998, *Praying with Power,* Christian Publishing House Yaounde-Cameroon.

www.ingramcontent.com/pod-product-compliance
Lightning Source LLC
Chambersburg PA
CBHW070404240426
43661CB00056B/2531